God Has the Answer, but What Was the Question?

R. E. King

God Has The Answer But What was the Question?
by R.E. KING

Printed in the United States of America

ISBN 9781624197307

Unless otherwise indicated, Bible quotations are taken from New King James version of the Bible. Copyright © 1982, by Thomas Nelson, Inc.

www.xulonpress.com

Table of Contents

This symbol represents author testimonies and/or comments.

Preface

One of the purposes of this book is to build a "perfectual" relationship. Perfectual relationships are ongoing encounters, communications with one who is perfect. There is no man that is perfect; therefore it would be a relationship with God. Oh, by the way, perfectual relationship is a phrase that Jesus gave me.

Although I am being used as the scribe on this work, I've received an incredible blessing in many directions. God showed me a spider web and told me that a network not unlike a spider web of connecting and interconnecting relationships would be developed because of this book. He told me it was necessary for God's people to share how and what and where God has affected their lives. Simply put, testimonies are one of the most powerful tools God is constantly giving to us to invest in other lives for the kingdom. For the record, the Bible is without question our main source of seeking the truth. In no way do I wish to state or imply that it is a secondary source. The Bible is the written word of God, and we use it to prove or disprove all.

Question: Where are you going to use me this day Lord, and how am I going to serve you and your people?

Answer:

On August 4, 2009, I was in my living room seeking God and his truth through prayer and the word. I don't recall it being particularly different than any other day of seeking a greater truth and or direction from God. As it turned out the direction God sent me was new and challenging. Often after my studies, God would commonly nudge me with a particular place He would want for me to go, or person I should contact and pray for, or various concerns that he desired to be a priority that day. This morning that voice, that I had tuned my ear and heart to recognize over many years began working inside me (John 10:3–5, 14). The Lord said, "You're going to write a book." I was shocked at how clear of a directive this was and chuckled to myself about God's selection. I said to him that I was sure of his voice and if he said it, regardless of what I viewed as my lack of qualifications, He had chosen me. I asked what the book was to be about and He replied, "How and what I communicate to my people. You will ask this question of my people, 'What is the most significant dream, vision or leading God has ever given you and you knew it was God?'" He continued, "The answers given will be called bones, and you will collect bones and place them in the bone pile, and go out and collect more bones." I asked, "How will I know when I have enough bones?" He simply said, "I will tell you when there are enough; until that time, collect bones." There was no confusion about this directive that morning, so I went out and bought my first of three digital recorders that would be used in the bone collecting. I immediately began making appointments for interviews, and the bone pile grew. For your clarification when He told me I was just the bone collector. I further understood that I was not to start any serious writing until the time He told me to start. Until October 11, 2010, when He gave me the go-ahead to begin writing, I did not spend any significant time trying to write or organize this work. There were many times when I was given inspiration that I thought could be used; I would place them in my journal and go out and collect more bones. I was definitely clear on His request but had to be reminded as time passed that I was to obey the last standing order. I understood that in order to make this work the way He desired, and to achieve the outcome He desired, it must be of Him, and by Him. One of the more significant leadings God is giving me for this book is to keep it simple. That's important because the truth is simple: Jesus loves you and desires that you get to know Him. The rewards of this will be obvious. Things in your life will change, and you will start experiencing love, joy, peace, long-suffering, kindness, and goodness in many forms and portions that at times are without measure.

Introduction

The preface to this book explains the source of the testimonies, called bones, which make up much of the content. However, the title, *God Has the Answer, but What Was the Question?* was birthed out of the realization that Jesus has the answer and is the answer to every question. He responds in various ways to people, but He always has an answer.

With the exception of Section 1, the various answers given are presented and placed in categories for the sake of organization. Some of the testimonies have elements of more than one style of response from Jesus. They are placed in an order that is consistent with the Holy Spirit's leading to the author and presented in the category which seems most dominant.

The types of people who have presented the testimonies are as varied as pebbles in a rushing stream bed. You will relate to some more than others, as we all do with all humanity we encounter. Even though God's word never changes, His responses to us do. It is my prayer that you find inspiration, identification, and motivation in these testimonies to pursue Him and His truth with greater fervor. After all, life can be one big adventure, a ride if you will. As you immerse yourself in this work, I advise you to put your tray tables in the upright position, stow all loose items under your seat, and fasten your seatbelts securely. Your tour guide, the Holy Spirit, will answer any inquiries you might have along the way. He never withholds any good things from those who seek Him.

SECTION ONE: DIVERSITY

Question: Does God hear the prayers of others for me?

Answer:

Terry said, "My grandma prayed for me and planted seeds in my spirit. She said although I got high on drugs, she was high on Jesus and that represented the best high." I asked, "Well, what corner does He work on?" She said, "He is the cornerstone. He is greater than any earthly drug and He offers life while they offer you death."

Thank you Lord for grandmas, grandpas, moms, dads, friends, and just folks who take the needs of loved ones, acquaintances, and strangers to your feet daily. They are truly the backbone of the church.

Perhaps your story started somewhat like Terry's within a family member, friend or stranger. Perhaps you are curious about God. Maybe you want to know more. Read on . . .

Question: Can God really heal my abusive past and give me freedom?

Answer:

My name is Diane, and I am a 61-year-old woman who was raised in a very abusive non-Christian home. At 21 I met my husband to be, Arnie, and his family. Arnie had been brought up in a Christian, loving home and brought some of those attributes into our marriage. At 22 we had one child; we were just living our lives, when a friend gave us the book *The Late Great Planet Earth* by Hal Lindsey. Shortly after reading the book I found out Hal was coming to our area for a conference. The book had drawn my interest, and we made arrangements for a babysitter. When the day came for the conference we went. I was sitting listening to Hal speak, and I was so touched. Arnie, I realized, had so much knowledge of Christianity, but I had none. For me, it was like I'd never felt anything even close to this; the Holy Spirit came down on me. At that very instant I felt God call me to come forward. Actually, both Arnie and I went forward without consulting each other; we were both called, Arnie to renewal and me to repentance. My life was changed at that instant, and I began a new journey in my home raising my children with the knowledge of Jesus.

 As I collected bones, I was often overwhelmed with God's love and desire to draw us to him. Romans 2:11 states there is no partiality with God. What that tells me is that He loves you and

me with equal, immeasurable, everlasting love, and I know there is no obstacle that He cannot or will not scale to draw us to Him.

Question: Is there someone who can help me love me?

Answer:

My name is Dave. I was about 10 years old and was a non-believer at the time; I had only been to church one time in my life. My dad was an agnostic, and my mother was a non-practicing Catholic. During this time in my life my dad was heavily involved in using and dealing drugs. I remember one night in particular: we were living in Portland, Oregon at the time, and I was saying prayers my grandmother from North Dakota had taught me to say before I went to sleep. I didn't necessarily know God; I was just saying them because I loved her, so I repeated the prayers that she had taught me. During this time from 8 to 10 years of age, I did as Grandma said, and in addition would ask God to help my family as she had also suggested. I was going through the ritual, and my dad was out in the living room. He had some people over, and they were snorting coke and smoking marijuana, and the music was loud, and they were loud. As I was finishing the prayer I looked up at the ceiling. My room was pitch black. All of a sudden with my physical eyes I saw angels that were floating above me, and I heard an audible voice say to me, "Dave, if you finish the prayer, I am going to take you with me, and you're going to fight with my army in Heaven. If you don't finish the prayer and you stop now, I am going to leave you here and there's going to be pain but I will make sure you're okay, all right?" As a ten-year-old boy, I heard this and was terrified. I had no idea what was going on. I saw this war in the heavens with angels fighting other angel-looking creatures, and I didn't know what to think. The audible voice freaked me out, and in the background, there was music and noise from my dad and his drug buddies in the living room; it was wild. I just didn't know what to do. Something inside me decided to finish the prayer. This voice that I assumed was God's would take me, and I would leave this world. I almost felt like, well it's better than the life I'm living now, so I finished the prayer and lay waiting. I was lying there and nothing happened. Pretty soon I realized I was not going anywhere. I tried to scream for my mom. I tried for what seemed about half an hour, but I was stricken with such fear and panic about what was going on that I couldn't even get a word out. Finally I was able to break this fear that was silencing me, and called to my mother. She came in and asked, "What's wrong?" I told her about this vision I just had, she broke down the started crying. She's apologized to me and said, "What you saw, that's from God, I haven't been living for God, and I'm so sorry that you have been exposed to this stuff. Don't ever forget what you saw and heard." My dad then came into the room. He was high, and let out a big sigh and said, "He's got a fever, he's just sleepy, he's just saying things." This whole episode didn't make a whole lot of sense when I was ten, but began making sense when I accepted the Lord as my savior at seventeen. It was at seventeen I realized that God through this weird visitation to a ten-year-old boy had prepared me. Although I didn't physically leave the planet, I remember that God used it, the visitation, throughout my years of rebellion and use of drugs and alcohol. He had his hand in my life, and one day He was going to call me to fight for him. God was calling me to be a part of his plan, and a part of his process of promoting the Gospel in the world. It was a message that told me the Lord was with me even at an early age. Between ages ten and seventeen when I was involved in dangerous behavior, He often would remind me of that supernatural encounter at age ten and I would somehow understand his hope for me, because that encounter was more real than anything in my life.

Question: Do I find the real God with my head or my heart?

Answer:

My name is Lorella, and I grew up in the basic Christian family during my formative years. I was nineteen years old when I had an epiphany; such a Spirit moved on me that I had to know God. Not just to hear about him; I had to know him. I began an odyssey that lasted about twenty-five years. I call those years the metaphysical years, metaphysical meaning beyond the physical. I searched in almost every major religion, this group, that group, I studied this, and I studied that, seeking anyone who seemed to have a line to God. I wanted to know God, and I wanted to know the truth. I was seeking truth, but of course eventually discovered the truth is God. What happened as I was doing this, was I learned a lot of things, and as soon as I felt satisfied that I had learned whatever was available from a certain group, I would be on to the next one. That continued until I was getting deep into meditative practices. Then suddenly one day God just stopped me, just like that! And I knew I could go no further. I knew I was not to continue on this path so I went into kind of a pause mode. Then, I read a book. The book talked about being born again and the baptism in the Holy Spirit with the manifestation of the gifts of the Spirit. Now, I asked myself, how I could go through twenty-five years of studying everything that I could get my hands on that seemed to lead to God or would get me closer to God, and miss all of what this book presented? It was soon that the day came when I said, "Jesus I want you to come into my life," because I had discovered, no one is going to get to God except through Jesus. I had been trying to come to God in other ways and further realized that many of the groups I had been involved in were in the same empty pursuit. They all had certain ideas about what was taking place, but it was usually not satisfying to me. I will never forget; I was in my room and I said, "Lord, come into my life, come into my heart." He then spoke to me because I had established a relationship with the Holy Spirit, one I had not realized at the time. He was guiding me out of the maze of deception into a true understanding of life in Jesus Christ. I called out, and God said, "Give me your life," just like that. He said it again, "Give me your life!" I had to think about that for a minute because when you are trying to maintain balance in your life you want to stay in control. I had to be very careful, but I finally said, "Lord I give myself to you." Immediately, it was like a bolt of lightning came through the ceiling, through me and through the floor. It was so powerful it completely changed my life. I was born again, and I knew it. I was in a completely different place. I was of the Spirit and not walking so much in the flesh. Before I was born again, I used to seek God and ask Him to let me be in His will. Even the meditative practices that I had gotten into ended as soon as I was born again. All barriers fell, and I had immediate and direct conversation with the Lord. He spoke to me and instructed me as to what I was to do. Within that same year, I was baptized in the Holy Spirit and spoke in tongues. It was as though He gave me a direct line to the Godhead. Since that time, He has guided me in ministry and in serving Him for some thirty-five years.

God welcomes us from lowly or lost places in our lives to His love and forgiveness. He invites us by saying, "Come to me and I will give you rest—all you who worked so hard beneath a heavy yoke. Wear my yoke, for it fits perfectly. Let me teach you for I am gentle and humble and you will find rest for your soul." (Matthew 11:28–30)

I believe most of us come from some kind of dysfunction, and if informed can be awed by the power God has to take something bad and change it and use it for good. Ken's story was one that seemingly had 100 percent chance of never changing. His was a case where the enemy had come to steal, kill, and destroy, but our God is a God of the impossible, and it pleases Him when we hear his voice through the chaos and respond. He is able to do anything.

Question: How did I get here? Am I in Hell? Is there a way out?

Answer:

My name is Ken, and my journey begins with the fact that I was born and raised in a military family, and we moved a lot. I've lived in foreign countries: Japan, Spain, Cuba, and in the United States in California and Virginia. I found out two years ago that my father was in military intelligence while I was growing up, which helps explain why things were so secretive and distant. When I was young my father was gone a lot, and my relationship with my mother was distant, and I had difficulty feeling any love. What ended up happening was as I grew older and started to mature, I started having dissociative identity disorders and panic attacks. I wasn't sure what they were at the time, so I went to get checked out because they were so severe. At that time medical professionals didn't know a great deal about this type of disorder. It is like emotional load on the mind becomes too big to handle, and situations are so extreme that you split, psychologically speaking, to other realities to escape. The best-known example of that situation would be the movie "Sybil" where a woman had sixteen personalities. Because the medical field was not offering me any kind of relief, I started using drugs and alcohol to kill the emotional pain. I didn't know any other way to cope. This first stage occurred between ages thirteen and fifteen. Along with the alcohol and drug problems came a bad attitude and a general disconnect from family. At that time we were living in Cuba on a military base, and I was having so much trouble that I was required to leave the base and live elsewhere. My life plunged down, and I began using anything and everything to relieve this painful experience. My parents lost control of me, signed me over to the state, and I ended up in a reform school in Idaho for about a year. That didn't change much. Although it removed me from the drugs and alcohol, it didn't change my attitude, and when I got out the behavior returned. That went on for about five years. I was expelled from school, spent time in jail, and didn't finish high school. All my friends were drug addicts, and alcoholics. Their lives were going downhill rapidly. One killed his grandmother; another killed a cop in a fight and is now imprisoned for life. Yet another overdosed on drugs and has permanent brain damage. When I was eighteen, I met a girl in Idaho and fell in love with her. As a result of that, I ended up hitchhiking from Idaho to the Seattle-Tacoma area of Washington state where the girl's parents let me live in the basement. That was a total blessing at the time, allowing me to get away from my old friends, lifestyle, and all the other chaos. My girlfriend's father gave me a job, and I worked hard, but I still had a drug and alcohol problem. This continued on for years. At twenty-nine I was married and had a daughter. But as in my previous life, I came to a point of desperation and something inside me said that my time had run out. I started having seizures from the alcohol, called a hospital, and told them my symptoms. They said I was most likely in the late stages of alcoholism and I needed to check into the hospital unit or I would surely die. I went to the alcohol unit, checked in, and began experiencing life free from the mask of alcohol and drugs that were just killing my emotions. When the garbage from the addiction wore off

I felt ten times as bad as I ever could remember feeling, and had a very hard time functioning in my new state. I was acting so crazy that the hospital considered just placing me in their psych ward's padded room. In that mental state, by God's grace, was the first time I reached out to God, because I knew that no human could help me and that drugs and alcohol were no longer an option. I got through that stretch in the early stages of rehab and attended AA for the next four or five years. I began feeling a little better, but the original problem came back, the dissociative disorder. I went to a therapist, who used New Age type techniques, and I felt some relief, feeling she understood some of my problems. As time went on, we had weekend retreats and got into weird stuff like soul retrieval, dark side, and astral travel. I didn't know at the time but it was just an open door for the ungodly. That went on for about a year. I was in my car one night on the way home from therapy thinking of much of my life experience saying things like, why this, why that, why, why, when a song on the radio caught my attention. The song said, "Show me how deep your love is." And it repeated the same line several times. I wasn't a Christian at the time but had been thinking of God and wanted to know what this love, this godly love, was all about. These thoughts and lines just remained in my head, and I couldn't get rid of them. So, I began sincerely asking God to love me and to expose me to this godly love. I began to feel something familiar even though I couldn't recall ever experiencing it quite like that before. I said: "God, just come down on me, give me all the love you have." Suddenly it felt like every cell in my body was filled with God's love and I just wept. I knew it was unconditional love from God. He didn't care about my past, and I could not contain what He gave me. It was over the top. For several days everything I viewed was from the perspective of this over-the-top infilling of love. Everything was new and fresh. I cried a lot and everything in my life that was horrible was just washed away. It made all the bad worth it just to have this experience with a loving God. Through this experience, I have listened to God's correction and direction in my life and I intend never to change the new life He is giving me.

It is now two years since I first heard Ken's testimony, and a year ago he enrolled in a ministry program in Redding, California and is growing and going strong for the Kingdom.

Question: Will you continue to use me in your miracles even if I don't see them coming?

Answer:

My name is Jeff and I'm a Christ-aholic I used to be able to go a half day without God's word. Now, I can't go without it for five minutes. On Christmas day, God asked me, by his Spirit, to go to the hospital and pray for a young man who had actually passed away on Civic Field but was then revived twenty minutes later. I called a brother in Christ, Dan, to come and pray with me for this kid. I really didn't know this young man well, but he had played football for me half of each of the last two seasons. Dan and I went up to pray for this young man. We didn't know a lot about his condition other than that he was in a coma and he was possibly waking up. When we arrived his girlfriend and his mother were already there by the bed. I talked to his mom, and she informed me that Patrick, her son, and some of his buddies had been out in the evening three days before Christmas and had done some coke and some drinking. They had jumped the locked fence at Civic Stadium and had been tossing passes around with the football. During that time, Patrick had just collapsed and stopped breathing. His friend had to jump the gate to get his cell phone from the car and call 911. A few minutes later the ambulance arrived and could not get in because the gate was padlocked. They found some bolt cutters and cut through the gate and drove the ambulance down to the field. This whole process took twenty minutes. The emergency medical team attempted to defibrillate him three times, and it didn't work. They were going to give up then decided to try one more time and Patrick came back to life but remained in a coma. When we went up to this room to pray for Patrick, I didn't feel like this was a big move of the Spirit. As I told my wife, I was asked to pray for this kid, and I thought it was going to be more for the comfort of his mom. Further it was what I was supposed to do because I was one of the leaders of the football team. Before I began praying, I laid my left hand on Patrick's head and grabbed onto his right hand. I just started praying and felt I could hear everybody's prayer both audibly and physically going through me. I was praying, and my left hand began to get very hot. Something happened—it was like supernatural. I can't really explain. Dan and I stopped praying, and he looked over at me, and I looked at him, and Dan said he thought

Patrick was lifted off the bed. I told him that I didn't know exactly what had just happened. Dan looked at me and said, "Let's get out of here." We turned to leave, and Patrick's best friend Aaron, who had been on the field there with Patrick, passed us as we left. The next day was the day after Christmas, and I went back just to see how Patrick's mom was doing because I felt I had actually made a connection with her. She said that her son got healed yesterday. I remembered back to the previous day when I saw Patrick; his eyelids would open, his eyes were rolled back, and there was no recognition. His best friend Aaron was in the room too, and he told me that yesterday when he walked past Dan and me and went into the room, as he walked to the bed, Patrick stood up out of the bed and gave him a hug and asked what had happened. He said that Patrick could only stand a short while and then had to lie back down. As a result of what happened that day, Aaron and Patrick's mother gave their lives to the Lord.

Patrick's prognosis was that it would be a couple of months before they would know if there was any brain damage. Further, it was stated that there would be at least three weeks of intense physical therapy to allow him to walk. Two days after this prognosis he was out of intensive care, and two days after that he was released from the hospital. He was given three days of physical therapy and on January 2, he was lifting weights and working out.

If you know Jesus, it will encourage you to reflect on and share how you met Him and how that has affected your life. Testimony does not belong to

25

us alone; it is meant to be shared. If you do not know Jesus, it is my prayer that as you visit these pages, He will introduce himself to you. I am convinced that He will make a way for you. Maybe there is a Bible available at your home, but if not, it is certainly online. Go to John 3:16, and He will reveal how much he loves you and will talk to you about your eternity.

SECTION TWO:
PROMPTINGS AND RESCUE

After completing the introductory section of this work, I hit a blank wall. I had a stack of precious bones, but was at a loss as to which way to proceed. I prayed, "Lord help me." My goal was not to just finish the book, but to complete it in God's order. I needed a supernatural guidance beyond my own 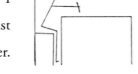 thinking. Almost immediately the word, "useful" came to me, and with it the understanding. In the beginning God told me to keep it simple, so that people like me could understand His purposes. I was told that this was a book of encouragement for the masses, not at all for the complex theological mind. That in fact, they may consider it foolishness. This was just for "us," you and me, struggling to overcome the sometimes, often times, difficulties of the human condition. Thankfully we don't have to do this alone, but with a creator who is prompting, calling, directing, guiding, and encouraging us every step of the way. We must stop and quiet ourselves, so we can seek and listen.

The Lord encourages us in Psalm 46:10 to be still and know that He is God. Often it is hard for us to be quiet because our flesh is full of energy and wants to do. I assure you that if you will spend time with Him just listening for His voice, He will speak and give you great revelation and guidance. Jesus is our example, and in the word (Luke 6:12) God shows how Jesus renewed His spirit and mind and how He would get himself in a position to receive godly inspiration and information, getting alone before God.

The Bible says in Acts 16:25 Paul and Silas prayed and sang from prison and the other prisoners heard them. I submit that God did too and it's reported in the next verse, Acts 16:26.

In Matthew chapters 5 through 7, possibly the greatest single sermon recorded, certainly the longest, Jesus said we should ask, seek and knock, and then He will answer. However, then we must be still and listen. Not all answers are earthquakes like the one Paul and Silas experienced.

The Word of God is the answer, and the Word became flesh (John 1:14). After Jesus returned to the Father, He said that He would send the comforter, the Holy Spirit. The Spirit would clarify and give us the Father's good plan for our lives, and if I may, guide us into the abundant gifts He wants to pour into our lives.

So, as you read, keep it simple! Take time to be still before God. It is easy to be distracted by the noise of this world. As living breathing humans, we often forget the first love things He has given and we only lean on our understanding. Proverbs 3:5 tells us to trust in the Lord with all our heart, and lean not on our own understanding. Oh how we must somehow return to the first excitement of knowing a Savior who makes us an overcomer. The secret is not complicated. Just put your one with Him. Jesus invites us to an intimate relationship. Intimacy is a one-on-one thing. I can tell you that every moment spent with Him will yield lasting peace, wisdom, purpose, and direction to you. I say this because this relationship is where we receive all the proper tools to live and love our way through this life. Just talk to Him. He desires to be closer than a friend. So, as you read, keep it simple! Take time, be still before God, and ask: what part of what you read is useful? Ask what truth can you obtain and use to take the next step of relationship with God? Is this place worth the precious time you have allotted me? Go to the Word, confirm what you're hearing, glorify Him, and continue. The Holy Spirit is so critical in this process of hearing God. He was sent by God to aid and comfort us as we walk and serve. That voice often is the voice of God through His Spirit.

Question: Is this an average day in Kingdom living?

Answer:

Some days God gives me special assignments. As is normal, generally, I study and pray and listen before leaving my home. I determined this morning that my first stop would be for a cup of hot coffee. As I considered which of several places I would stop for coffee, I was prompted by what time and experience had taught me was the Lord's voice. This voice was loudand clear within me. He said, "I want you to go to the McDonalds on Burnham; there will be a redheaded woman in

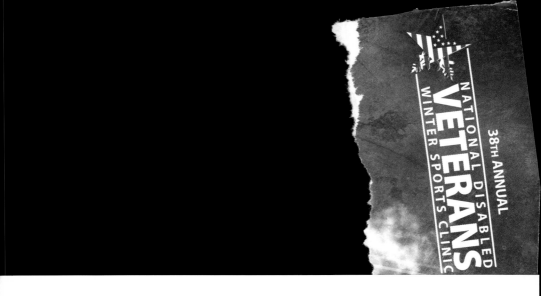

need of a healing prayer. If you will lay hands on her and pray for her in My name, she will be healed." Well, I thought, this sounds like a unique way to start a day, so I drove to McDonalds and went inside. After checking the sparse populace inside, including employees, no redhead was found. I determined that I had either been delusional, or she had not arrived yet. Opting to trust the instruction I took my Bible out, sat down in a booth and read and drank coffee. Approximately fifteen minutes passed, and I realized someone had taken a seat in the booth behind me. I knew before turning around it would be my assignment. I turned and sure enough it was a glowing redheaded woman. I stood and addressed her: "Hello, my name is Ralph." I extended my hand to shake hers, and she reciprocated with her hand, with an obvious confused look on her face. I explained that I was a man of God and that God had sent me to pray for a redheaded woman who was in need of a healing. I asked, "Would that be you?" Having her complete attention at this point she replied, "Funny you should ask, I have been having extreme back issues and right now my back is killing me!" I wasn't surprised by her response because from the moment I laid my eyes on her the Lord had been confirming in me that this was in fact the woman I was to pray for. About this time her significant other, a young man, sat down in the booth across from her and remained silent. I continued, "May I lay hands on you and pray for you?" She said yes. I was aware that her significant other's eyes were alertly on me, but I felt no threat. I put my hands on her back and prayed a simple prayer for healing in Jesus' name. We did not talk long other than to receive a brief introduction of the significant other. I thanked her for allowing me to pray for her and left, assignment complete. What, you're saying to yourself, didn't you engage them or her further? That seems strange, you might be thinking. As I experienced it, I thought it strange that I didn't ask a few obvious questions. The answer was simple. God did not lead me to do anything further. My job was done, and I could trust the outcome to Him.

A caution to you: if you choose to follow an instruction given to you by God, don't alter it. This, my brothers or sisters, is one of the most important directives I can give you. You can remain in a wilderness for an extended period of  time if you put your plan above His. Israel's exodus and trip to the Promised Land is a great example of altered routes, which could have been much shorter and less painful had they followed God's instruction. An example I had during the collecting of bones for this book went as follows. After approximately ten weeks of collecting bones I awoke on a Tuesday morning to what can only be described as disorder of the mind, a lost state. God seemed at least distant, and I felt uneasiness on the border of panic. I cried out for relief and heard through the clamor that I was to contact and meet with a pastor friend at his church in Olympia and ask for his council. I called this otherwise very busy man who said he would be happy to see me because he had just experienced three cancelations in his schedule, and it was wide open for the next three hours. I told him I was on my way and arrived at his office about an hour later. We talked for a while on unrelated issues, and then I did my best to explain my condition. He remained silent for what seemed an extended time and then said: "I've been praying since you called, not knowing what you were bringing and now after hearing the explanation of your state, I am prompted to ask, has God given you a special assignment?" I replied that yes, He is having me write a book. I told him that I was collecting testimonies, which God called bones and when I had a sufficient amount, He had showed me he would breathe life into them, put skin on them, and they would be a living testament to His power and glory. In the process of explaining what God had assigned me, he also made me aware of my problem. Yes I had done as God said in collecting the bones; however, in the process of collecting I had come across some favorites that spoke to me in a more personal way. Instead of placing them in the bone pile and going out and collecting more until He said there was enough, I had created my own special pile that I would go back to and bask in what was His glory and not mine. I explained my plight to the pastor, we prayed, I repented, and I left delivered and prepared to collect the next bone.

Question: Can God be involved in our decision making?

Answer:

I spent four years at the Westin Hotel Company as a sales executive in their Scottsdale, Arizona office. I remember vividly that the same time I was constantly hearing and writing tunes and lyrics both in my mind and on paper. As I said, I was working in corporate America so there was a position that was coming available that I had spent a few years pursuing within the Westin Company. It was the very top position. I was in an executive sales position, and the next would be the team leader of the executive sales staff. It was the most coveted position in the company, and I was pursuing the things of this world through this, even though I was going to church, singing on the worship team, and producing my first album. I remember thinking I want to follow the Lord with more of myself. A good friend and mentor of mine named Jim called and told me that the Lord had given him a vision regarding my future. He asked if I would meet him for breakfast, and I said sure. Jim had heard some of my music that I have been working on in the studio and generally knew about me, so I was looking forward to this meeting. We got together the next morning for breakfast—I love chili cheese omelets—so I'm sitting there gorging myself on this huge omelet, and I'm so excited that he was going to share with me about what God had told him. Instead of talking about it, he just scoots a piece of paper across the table in front of me. It looked like a spreadsheet, and one side says "Pursuing Income" and the next column says "Pursuing Ministry." It had all the benefits of pursuing an income in one column like, gain, power, or ability to own, blah, blah, blah. On the pursuit of ministry, there was a column that had things like, eternal ramifications—you know, like people's lives changed forever and on and on. I told him it was interesting. He said the Lord showed him that I needed to choose. Here I was pursuing this work life and earning $200,000 a year, and that was pretty good for me. I was in the top one percent of the company, and I'd won the awards, and they had sent me to Greece and Italy and all over, first-class everything, and I just had this real nice life. My income was going to more than double by taking the new job because they had just announced to me that I had been selected for the position that I had dreamed of and pursued since starting with the company. All I had to do is just wait for thirty more days, and it was mine. I was at a crossroads. I had been pursuing an income, but the Lord had been preparing me to pursue ministry. I began praying in earnest about this. I said, "Lord if it's your will for me to pursue a ministry, then help me to see that direction, help me to know what choices to make or not to make to move toward your will. I'm asking to see your clear direction and that I would be empowered to go that way because my desire is to serve you." When I made that declaration before the Lord he began to redirect my focus to the things that were pure and clean and lovely, away from those things that were monetary and superficial and shallow. As my focus was redirected, the Lord showed me that he wanted me to put a notice in at work. Everyone there thought I was crazy because I was giving up this half a million dollar a year job, because at the time that's what the best in that position were making, and since I was training those people, I knew if I turned down the position that the very person I trained up would take it in my place. That made it even more difficult of a choice, but looking back at my choice—and although my family and myself have gone through trials and struggles the past two years—we have learned to trust the Lord as our provider in a greater way than any ability I might have to provide for us. I have moved from a point of self-sufficiency to a position of totally surrendering to the Lord as our provider. He is everything I need; I don't need to worry how these things are going to come to pass; I just need to focus on him. My wife and I have grown in our faith tremendously as we were forced, in a sense, to trust on the Lord for every single provision. I prayed, "Am I to stay, am I to go," and was listening intently because the Lord gave a new focus, and I didn't want to miss this direction; otherwise giving up the job made no sense. "What is your will Lord"?" I said, and He said, "Go to Washington state." Then I said, "Okay Lord, when am I to go?" He said, "Move now!" I said, "Okay, but Lord you are going to have to show my wife because I can't do it without her." I had already told my wife that the Lord wanted us to move to Washington. She had said that she was not going there: the kids are still in school, all our friends are in Arizona, and my whole family is in Arizona. I told her we should just pray about it. "Then, when He reveals it to you we will move to Washington," she said that was just arrogance and pride, and I said, "Okay; maybe it is, but let's just pray about it." So being the good woman she is, she began praying, and I repeated my prayer once again that "if this is of you Lord then reveal it to her." Shortly after that conversation with my wife I had an opportunity to do a ministry event in Washington at a prison with the Christian Motorcycle Association. At the close of that event an altar call was given and about 100 people came forward for salvation. I couldn't help recalling the scripture which states that "The harvest is plentiful but the workers are few." I said at that point, "Lord I want to be one of the workers; send me and I will go." After that event I went to my parents' house in Port Orchard, Washington, and while there, the Lord spoke to me and said, "Move here." I asked, "Do you mean here, here, at my parents' house?" I heard it again, "Move here!" I'm a good provider, we're living in the million dollar house, I have fancy cars, a fancy life; everything I ever desired in the world. This worldly thinking gave way to the truth back in Arizona. I had nothing because I was a slave to my job; I was climbing the corporate ladder only to find myself used, abused, and empty. Going to Port Orchard presented the appearance of giving up everything. On top of everything, the idea of moving in with my parents proved that the Lord's ways are not always our ways. I returned home to Arizona and after a hard day's work and giving my notice, there she was; my wife. The kids were in bed, the candles were lit, and the mood was set. She just smiled at me, and I perceived the sense of peace that replaced the uneasiness that she had felt before at my pursuing the Lord's will. There she was looking at me across the table and then she said that during the day something interesting happened to her. "I started to pray about Washington and I think God wants us to go to Washington," she said. "I'm so sorry that I have been holding you up as you follow God's vision for us." She continued, saying, "Today I just started getting excited about what I don't want to do and that's how I know it's the Lord. He wants us to go to Washington and I am willing to go wherever you want to go because he showed me He is going to lead you and I'm just blown away by it. This dinner is to represent that the Lord spoke to me, and I can see clearly now what His vision is . It's an amazing one, and I don't want to mess it up." I sat there and it was like, you have got to be kidding me, the perfect God orchestrating the perfect answer.

Question: Can we receive real freedom and live in jail?

Answer:

I went to court with a kid in my youth group who had a traffic violation. When I got in the courtroom I sat down and noticed a guy that had walked in behind me and sat down behind me. His hair was slicked back, he was wearing a jean jacket, and he looked kind of rough.

God gave me a word for him, but I couldn't say anything because it would have been disruptive, and you must be quiet. So I slid him a note that said, "My name is Dave. You don't know me; please give me a call. God spoke something to me about you, and I want to share it." I handed him the note; he read it and gave me crazy look. The following day, Wednesday, while sitting in my office at New Beginnings in Portland, Oregon, where I served as a youth pastor, the guy called me and he said, "I'm Brian; I'm the guy you slipped the note to; what's up?" I said, "This may sound very weird to you, but the Lord told me to tell you that whatever was in your dad is in you, and also the Lord said that your dad is dead to you. I don't know whether he's dead in your heart or whether your dad died; that's all I heard. But I do know this God has a plan, and He wants to break you out of this situation that links you to your dad and the negativity that has come from your dad." There was a big pause of silence on the phone, and I thought he hung up on me, but then he said, "Who are you and how do you know me?" I said, "I never met you in my life; I just walked into the courtroom like you. I'm a believer and a pastor and I felt God speak those words to me." He responded, "The last words I spoke to my dad were, 'You're dead to me' and two weeks later he killed himself by shooting himself in the head with a shotgun. My dad was a violent drug addict, and I'm a violent drug addict. I just got out of jail because some years back I shot and killed my best friend, and I'm coming up on parole." I pleaded, "Please come to church tonight; just come and hear about God." He said he didn't believe in God but perhaps he might stop by. So he came that night with his girlfriend. I met him at the door; he shook my hand hard, convict style, and he looked at me, checking me out like somehow I was shady and he doesn't buy what I was saying." He sat in the back, and all night he was just glaring at me the whole service. I preached on the love of God, and at the end of that service he came up to the altar and he got on his knees with his girlfriend. He was crying like a baby and gave me a big hug. That night he received Jesus in his heart, and he would be returning to jail, free and forgiven.

Question: Can He give me what I do not desire and then cause me to fall in love with it?

Answer:

Two years ago another pastor on staff was unable to go on a mission trip to Africa and asked me to go in his place. Although I am an African-American pastor, I absolutely had nothing for Africa. I didn't care about Africa and had too much I was doing here. I was focused on what God had for me here; however, the Holy Spirit kept prompting me to attend a class on Swahili. He just brought me along inch by inch until I had fallen off the edge and said finally, ""Okay, I'll go."" We got to Africa and were riding the bus from the airport to the YWAM base. Looking out the window at my first view of Africa, the Holy Spirit spoke to me and said, "The only hope for Africa is the church and the only hope for the church is discipleship." The Spirit continued, "You are going to do a pastor's and leadership conference here but don't say anything to anybody until they ask." By the end of the week, I had run into a pastor that scheduled a meeting for me to speak in his church. When he spoke to me he looked at me, with prophetic eyes, and said to me, You are supposed to do pastors and leadership conference here." I said, in my head, okay God this is a setup. I preached at a number of different churches, and there was tremendous knowing and favor. It was amazing because it felt almost like home. After leaving there, I was just blown away at what God was doing. On the way back on the plane, God gave me another Download, as I call them. He said every year you're going to do pastors and leadership conference and in 2013 you're going to establish training and equipping center in Africa. I thought yeah, okay, that's definitely a stretch. I came home and in my debriefing with my executive pastor I told him what God told me. He looked at me and said "Felix, that sounds like God to me; let's make it happen." I looked at him and said to myself are you kidding me? Then I met with my senior pastor and told him the exact thing I had told my executive pastor. He told me, "I knew God was going to rock your world over there; let's make that happen." I went home and said to my wife that I had been ready for someone to tell me that's just post-mission euphoria. You need to get back with me six months because that's a little crazy. Nevertheless no one told me I was crazy except for my wife, who did tell me I was crazy.

Question: Will you prepare me before I go, Lord?

Answer:

I recently joined the staff of a church after years of being in ministry. As such, it has been a change because I used to have daily contact with those who were not Christians, and now I have to look for people who are not. I find that to be challenging. One of the women who is on staff at the church asked me to talk to her husband, who is not a believer. I was upfront with Dale and told him I'd like to talk to him about becoming a follower of Jesus Christ. He told me he was a hard case, and I assured him that I had heard that but that God didn't need me to defend Him. I told him I just wanted to hear his heart and tell him why I follow Jesus and make a case why he should consider the same. I wish I could say today that there was a conclusion to that, but we have been meeting regularly for about a month and a half. He has yet to make a commitment to Jesus but is studying, and we are praying together. I believe that Jesus, who loves him, will find a way. What I want to convey is how God led me in that first meeting. I sought counsel from other people; I prayed and was impressed that the first meeting would have very little to do with what I had to tell Dale but how I needed to listen to him. The only word given when I prayed was "doubt," which I wrote down on a tablet. In our first get together, we had some small talk, and kind of a howdy time. Finally, I said, "Well Dale, I'm not here to convince you to be anything. I'm simply here to ask you first of all where are you in your thinking and what is it about a walk with Jesus that you find difficult. The first words out of his mouth were, "I'm not a guy like you who doesn't doubt." It was absolutely amazing to me that the one word in the English language that God had prepared me to talk about was the very first word he mentioned. He had prepared me to discuss that with him and explore it further. I was able then to show Dale and convince him that it was God who was leading our discussion. It was not me, and God was going to reveal himself to Dale as he sought Him. I explained that God promised that those who seek God will find Him. Every meeting—the discussions, the questions that Dale asks—are things God has dealt specifically with me days or even hours prior to our meetings. God has prepared me for the very questions that Dale is going to ask, and there is no doubt in my mind that as we pursue to seek and save, this will occur. Not that we are doing the saving ourselves, but He will prepare us with the right knowledge and words.

Question: Can the Lord give us a second chance to be obedient?

Answer:

I was in my late twenties, and I was working for a restaurant company in the Midwest. I had observed that at work most of the supervisory staff was wearing jewelry, and I thought it would be kind of cool if I bought a ring. I did so and thought it was a little overboard, but I wore it some. It really wasn't that important to me, but I felt pretty cool about it. I was working with Sambo's and within about eighteen months or so

I was promoted to district manager and went around and did pancake breakfast promotions. At the same time, my wife and I were attending a big church in Ft. Wayne, Indiana. The church was in the building process to add a big, new addition. The Lord led me, and I really felt like perhaps I should have given that ring to the building fund. I argued with myself and said just let it go because I didn't need it. I hesitated and didn't give it but instead hung onto it. A few months later I was up in Detroit, Michigan doing promotions and stayed in a hotel overnight. After getting dressed, I forgot the ring on the nightstand. I realized at about 10 or 10:30 AM that the ring was not on my finger, where it should be, and I sped back to the hotel. I talked to the manager, who got a hold of housekeeping, but no ring. There's no way, I knew what had happened; it was gone. I should've given it, didn't give it, and now it was gone. Well I prayed about that and felt really bad about it because I knew the Lord had impressed on me to give that ring. I happened to be back in Detroit a couple months later and decided I'd swing by the motel and see if that ring was ever returned. I went in and talked to the manager and he asked me to describe the ring to him. I did and he began to tell me a story. He said, "About a week after you were here the girl who had worked that room and had taken that ring got to feeling guilty about it, decided not to pawn it, and brought it back in to me. I have been holding it just in case someone ever came back to claim it." He gave it back to me and the next Sunday morning it went straight into the offering. I knew that was something I was supposed to do originally, and He gave me a second chance to be obedient.

Question: Is what I envision and what you call me to do always a surprise?

Answer:

My name is Kevin, and I am an elementary school teacher. I felt a strong calling in my life years ago to work with kids. I answered that call and became a public school teacher. In the last couple years, God has added something to my heart. I've never seen myself as a leader or teacher of men. Never. But it started with me asking God to plug me into a men's group. In response, the Holy Spirit whispered to me to start a group, so I did. About a year and a half ago after teaching Sunday school one morning and experiencing extreme frustration while working with kids I felt were broken, I realized, I often worked with parents that were broken also. As a release from my frustration, I decided to go for a bike ride. While riding, I asked God how I could reach these kids. His response was immediate. He said, "If you want to reach these children you must first reach their fathers." Like I said, I never had seen myself as a leader of men, but it appeared that God was building a place for it in my life. I was leading this men's group, and now I had this strong desire to teach children but to also reach men: fathers. It was a yearning to teach men in this broken society that we as men are to take back our children and our families from this world. It's become a vision and mission in my life to reach these men all around me to teach them to be the fathers and husbands that God intended them to be. I have realized that all that is needed of you to serve God is to say yes, pray, and follow God's leading.

Question: Can one more hot dog change my life?

Answer:

When I was in high school I had occasion to enter a hot dog eating contest. There were two other guys in it that I knew. One was a football player from my school, and the other was a guy, Brian, I knew from youth group at church. I just got in the contest myself because I wanted a free hot dog so after a couple I bailed out. This football player just kept eating and eating and I thought he was going to win the contest because he already consumed fifteen hot dogs. But I realized at some point that this other guy from my youth group was doing as well as a football player. Prior to this realization while still sitting next to the football player, he handed me a hot dog under the table and I took it. Well, before I knew it the contest was down to the football player and my friend from youth group. It turned out that the football player won the contest by one hot dog and received $100 prize, which in those days was a lot of money. I felt convicted as to my part in taking away the win from Brian, and the next day I went to his house and knocked on the door. Brian answered. I told him that he really didn't lose the contest and explained what I had done. I said, "To make this right I'm going to give you $100." So I did. The whole point is that the conviction of my act and the leading by the Holy Spirit to correct it was huge.

Question: Do wise, godly parents make a difference?

Answer:

I've been serving God my whole life. There wasn't a turning point, per se, where I all of a sudden accepted Christ. My relationship is more like my relationship with my dad; it's has always been there. When people ask me how long I've known the Lord, that's like asking "How long have you known your dad?" I have great parents who taught me about God from a very young age. I think the first time God really spoke to me it was on the concept of grace, unmerited favor, and the idea of forgiveness for sin. I was five or six years old when this concept was presented to me. In my home we did spankings, and I'm a firm believer in spankings. On this occasion I had done something wrong; I don't even remember what it was. I'd been sent to my bedroom by my mom and dad, and I was waiting on my bed, dreading their arrival. My mom and dad came in and I was fully expecting that I was going to be beat. Instead my dad came over and sat next to me on the bed and said, "You know what you did was wrong and there's no getting around it, you deserve punishment. But we are going to do it different this time. I am going to take your punishment; you do not have to be spanked." Then instead of my dad spanking me he bent over the bed and my mother spanked my dad. I sat there and watched my dad be punished for something I did wrong. My dad started crying and mom even started crying. There was no shortage of tears—mine were included. That day the concept of grace and mercy was planted and began to make some sense to me. At that place and time I started to feel a healthy sense of regret for doing things wrong. I started to understand that when I do things wrong it didn't just affect me; it could do things to my mom and dad also. It began to solidify a clarity of understanding that disobedience and sin: while I may have to deal with punishment, there is another side. I could not imagine how much it hurts my Father in heaven. I believe my understanding of sin and grace began in that bedroom, and the journey goes on.

Question: Where's God's fit for me?

Answer:

When I was eighteen years old, I started junior college, and my general attitude was that I was just following the crowd. I went two years to junior college and said, "Well that wasn't that hard; I will go onto a four-year college." It was a teacher's college, so I thought well I'll become a teacher; that seems like a pretty good job. So I went to college, and my first teaching assignment was rough to say the least. I thought, what have I gotten myself into? I tried switching and taught a different grade and a different level, and that first assignment lasted about five years. My thinking was maybe this isn't for me, perhaps I should try another approach; I have taught in public schools, so why not try a Christian school? I taught at a Christian school for a year and it turned out to be one of my hardest years, and at the end I felt like I got kicked out. I thought, well maybe teaching is not my thing;

I've been teaching for five or six years and it doesn't seem to work for me. During this same time period I married my husband, Jim, and had an opportunity to go to a Bible college, so I said that sounds good and went. Shortly after graduating from the Bible college, Jim and I began attending a new church. Jim told me that the church needed teachers in their school. I said, are you kidding me? Been there, done that. He said, "No, no, no, go there; they need teachers." I finally agreed, with the understanding that since I had not taught in the classroom for a number of years, I would serve as a volunteer, not a full-time teacher. I came home that afternoon after talking to the school administrator, and said to Jim, "She hired me." For the next eighteen years I taught first grade and found out that first day, beyond a shadow of a doubt, the moment I stepped into that room I was called. I came from a place where my experiences in the classroom had intimidated me to a point of being totally confident about where God placed me. I kept my eyes on Jesus those eighteen years and taught Bible and had those kids just eating out of the palm of my hand. God had inspired me to feed them fresh manna from his Word each day. Different times through the years when life offered its problems, I asked God, "Is this where I should be?" He has assured me that he had designed me for this and that I was where I should be, so I joyfully carried on.

Question: How do we know the way to go when we are at a crossroad?

Answer:

I will tell you of a crossroads in my life that had to do with our whole future. I was between my fourth and fifth year in Bible college in the Midwest and had no idea where we were going upon graduation or, for that matter, what we would be doing. When college was over and all the other students had gone home, we still had no idea what we were going to be doing or where we were supposed to be in this world. We lived in a humble little place that had a spacious backyard, and one night, still not knowing what or how or where we were going, I raised my hands to a star-filled heaven and said, "Where do we go from here?" As I was praying, I noticed about 100 yards down the street under a street lamp, sat a little white cottontail rabbit and I said, "God if we are to go to Washington state could you bring that little rabbit by me?" The cottontail turned around, came right toward me, entered into the shadows, and stopped at my feet. As he stopped, I had an involuntary jerk, and he sped away into the darkness. I thought, well that can't be from God. I'm sure it just happened. Then I said, "Oh God if you want me to go would you bring that rabbit back to me one more time?" Then out of the darkness to where I stood that cottontail came and sat right by my feet. I was convinced! But we had no car—we had used it to pay our college bills—we had a new little girl, and knew no one who lived in or would be traveling to Washington. Near this time my wife had been reading in the paper. She looked up and said, "Look here, a man named Clyde Chapman from Joplin has a car that he wants driven to Washington state." So I called and made an appointment to meet with him and took the bus sixty minutes from Springfield to Joplin. Sure enough he said, "You are just the man I'm looking for." He had confidence that was unexpected given I could hardly grow whiskers, but regardless he lined up the money for gas and the vehicle, and we loaded that car to the top with all our worldly possessions and our precious little girl jammed in the front seat between us in a bassinet. We started God's adventure for our lives. Now after fifty years of serving God in Washington, then to the mission field and eventually back to Washington, we are in our sunset years and continue this adventure.

Let me encourage you to stop reading and try an exercise that can be both revealing and helpful as you walk this walk. First write down the question God asked me to ask of believers.

WHAT IS THE MOST SIGNIFICANT DREAM, VISION, OR LEADING THAT YOU HAVE BEEN GIVEN AND YOU KNEW IT WAS GOD?

Now, write what comes to mind. Some assistance for those who have many significant encounters with God would be to perhaps write the first and the last. I can't encourage you enough to do this; there will be renewal and a power surge as you put in print those treasures that God has given you.

My Bone:

_____

_____

_____

_____

_____

_____

_____

_____

_____

_____

_____

_____

_____

_____

_____

_____

_____

_____

_____

During the next week ask God for the opportunity and boldness to share this "bone" with a person of His choice.

God offers all kinds of correction, direction, and guidance to teach and prepare us to pay it forward, that is, to invest in future generations for the Kingdom. You have already read many examples of how God communicates with us; some are life directives and others profound miracles. These are designed by Him to encourage and mature the saved and to convince the lost that He is a God of today; a living, loving God who desires that none should perish.

Contained in some of the following bones are bigger steps, ones that perhaps may be difficult for us to advance toward without God's assurances. No matter what God has, or is, or will call you to do, He will also provide a way. The key is stepping out of the boat, or moving closer to God is trusting and keeping our mind on Him. Along the way limited thinking is commonly our stumbling block, when in fact God has no limits. We tend to think too small and not remember that we serve the God that created the heavens and the earth and that He is greater and bigger than any challenge we might face. To combat this shortcoming personally, I explore the Word and pray, but do it with an expectation of greater things. I frequently launch that thinking with a familiar song lyric, "I won't be satisfied with anything ordinary." Think beyond your circumstance and trust your unknown future to a known God. God promises never to leave us or forsake us (Heb. 13:5). Proverbs 18:24 speaks of a friend (Jesus) who sticks closer than a brother.

Question: Is there a plan and purpose?

Answer: It's as easy as ONE-TWO-THREE.

ONE

I was at a church youth camp and that was the summer I got filled with the Holy Spirit. I remember having a distinct feeling that that experience would be translated into me serving the Lord. I never thought of myself as a pastor, preacher, counselor, or any of the things I am today. But there wasn't any doubt that I was called to serve. At that time it meant I was into more service stuff like carrying tables to set up for banquets or putting together a little youth choir or just service oriented tasks.

TWO

I was seventeen, it was Christmas, and my grandmother and step-grandfather were visiting from California. My grandfather served there as a pastor. On that Christmas visit my grandmother looked at me and said, "Gary, I think the Lord is going to make you a preacher." Although I was playing baseball, graduating from high school, and thinking of four million other things, that prophetic word never left me. That piece of God's puzzle for my life always remained in my mind, and when I changed majors in college from business to social work, it once again came to my mind and remained.

THREE

At age fifty-six, I was in charge of an assisted living facility; that was approximately five years ago. My senior pastor at the time was planning his transition into retirement. The pastor that God had chosen—but had not yet been selected to fulfill that void—and I were walking down a hallway, and he said, "You know Gary, when I am senior pastor," (which was his own piece of prophecy), "I want you to come on board with the church and do counseling." At that moment I knew it was the Lord revealing the next step in my path. When I look back at my life and experiences that prepared me for the position I now hold, there is no doubt it was orchestrated by the Lord in a variety of ways. It all comes together as I sit here in the counseling chair now, but that moment when the pastor said, "Gary this is where I want you." I knew it was from the Lord.

Question: When God calls us, is it okay if it's something that's cool?

Answer:

My life has been a constant growing experience. I grew up in a Christian home and was very fortunate to have parents that sacrificed to make it possible for me to have a Christian education all the way through college. For a while you could say my faith was my parents' faith. It took time for me to get where it was my personal relationship with my God. The standards I have now are not so different than the ones I grew up with; it's just that they're much more personal. For me it's not something that happened overnight. I can see looking back now how God guided my past in order that I might be who I am today. I was about fifteen years of age when I began taking interest in playing the drums. I think the main reason was, I was playing the trumpet at the time and the guys in the drum line just seemed way cooler. I became interested in drums and would sit down at a drum kit at any opportunity and just play. For a few years I played in the praise band in my youth group, and in the private school I attended, I played drums for the student-led praise and worship group as well. God just continued to build this desire and passion for music. The summer between my freshman and sophomore year of college was where I really struggled with where I needed to go next, where God wanted me to go next. I had been going to a university for a year and driving home on weekends. I just began questioning what God's plan was for me and I started praying and reading the Word for an answer. I came across two verses that spoke to me. They were Philippians 4: 6–7: "Be careful for nothing but in everything by prayer and supplication with thanksgiving let your requests be made known to God and the peace of God that passes all understanding shall keep your hearts and minds through Christ Jesus". That helped me so much. I didn't have to worry about what I was to do next; God had already started something in me that he would develop and use in the future. I believe that my decision to leave my college and pursue full-time music ministry at that time was truly a leading of God and a step of faith. I've learned being in a Christian band is not all it's cracked up to be: we break down on the road, sleep in the van, miss meals, and with all that some kid will come up to me after a show and say, "That song you just played just made me so happy; your smiling faces just make me want to be like you guys." And by that, God's opened the doors of opportunity. I remember one show two girls came up to us and they wanted us to know that they had accepted Christ that night. What a rush—the fact that God is using me in this ministry that humbles me. The fact that God still wants to use a twenty-three-year-old guy that messes up every day amazes me. He doesn't need me, but he loves me so much that he has given me the desires of my heart through music to spread the Word. It's a touching thing for me to be able to do what I love on a daily basis knowing that it could affect this generation as well as others. One of the countless times God has revealed himself was when we were playing a show in New York, and we met one of the stagehands who stated she was an atheist, and further, she wore a pentagram to prove it. This occasion was also the first time we were playing a ninety-minute set. After approximately forty-five minutes, we took a break and went backstage and saw that the woman we met was crying. We asked her what was going on, and she said, "Those words you were singing started something in me; they got me thinking about something I've never seen or heard before." We continued to talk to her, and she began to question, saying, "This is so different than I'm used to, so much different than I've ever heard." The whole band, the four of us, circled around her and began sharing and praying, and she accepted Christ as her Savior. For me wherever this ministry takes me I have decided to walk this road humbly,. I'm going to look at this opportunity to have more eternal impact on my generation.

Question: Will you allow me Lord, just another man, to make a difference?

Answer:

The one thing that jumps out to me that I believe is only known by two people. It sounds kind of bad sometimes, but it is financial. This occurred a few years back when a new pastor had been voted in as senior pastor. His vision for leadership included not just to being involved but being agents of change. I thought: I've got to be more than just a part; I have to be a change agent. I began praying about it, about making a change. I'm a giver by nature, so giving to me is not hard to do; it's something that comes quite easily. I thought, well in order for me to make a significant difference I could use some investments I had to make a change. I think that's primarily how God speaks to me. He gives me a thought and I think, "I've never thought that before," but I recognize it and realize it's the Holy Spirit speaking to me. The thought was that if I take these investments, and they would have to make incredible returns, I could make a significant difference. I knew from past experience with this type of investments that in order to accomplish what I wanted, it normally would take three or four years, but they were by far the best investments. If you told people about them they would appear as crazy investments with crazy returns. I decided if I was successful with these investments I would give half the investment back—not my normal 10 percent—but half. I thought if I could make $1,000,000 on this, 50 percent or $500,000 would go to the church for a proposed project. So time went on and these things did incredibly well. I had done investments before with the same group, that although others who had invested in had not been always successful, I somehow generally hit a home run and usually within three or four years, whatever goal I'd set was achieved. This time beforehand, I decided I would set up parameters as to how the final amount would be distributed. I would receive the money, pay any necessary taxes, and then give 50 percent of what was left. So, it was all set up, and I knew exactly my agreement with God and wouldn't start fudging. I knew that without this detailed commitment, I would or could start thinking my way around it. The short story is at the end of the day when the math was done after three years I gave $503,000 to the Lord for this project. The Lord allowed me, just another man, to make a significant difference.

Question: What must I do or change to show others my miracle God?

Answer:

I had a time in my life where I was just hungry to experience God in a deeper way. Maybe I had gotten complacent about my walk with Christ and wanted to experience the supernatural. I'd spent time in the book of Acts reading about miracles that God was doing. I guess I was a bit tired of trying to convince people about my Jesus. I wanted them to see that my God is alive and powerful and wanted God to use me in miraculous ways.

As I pursued this, God challenged me to turn off every other noise in my life, everything that could take up time and mental energy and focus. I was to give it to Him every second of the day that I could. What I did for the next two weeks was when I got up in the morning, I spent double time in prayer and then every time a new hour came up in the day, at twelve, one, two, etc., at the top of every hour I would spend ten minutes in prayer. So if I was driving, if I was in the mall, if I was anywhere alone I would do this. If I was in front of people involved in a situation I would pray in my head when possible. During this time I was really pressing my flesh through a grinder and was turning off every other noise in my life except for the Lord. My prayer was, Lord I want to be aware of what you're saying, and I want you to use me throughout my day in ways you want. I know I have just been tuning you out, especially outside the four walls of the church. I headed into the street and God began to do things. The first instance was driving down the road in a part of town I seldom travel. I was going to visit my mom. She worked in a hardware lumber store. On the way there I was listening to Christian radio, worshiping God, when all of a sudden the Lord placed in my spirit to turn off the radio and pray in the Spirit. I had been baptized in the Holy Spirit, and I was praying in tongues, and as I prayed I felt this urgency and began to pray almost like there was desperation within my spirit. I prayed with such intensity that I knew it was God putting a massive burden on my heart at that time. All of a sudden as I'm driving I feel a leading. I'm supposed to go to the left to go to my mom's work but I feel this leading to turn right into a McDonald's. I pulled into the McDonald's; I don't know why I'm pulling in, I'm praying in the spirit and I feel a major burden on my heart. As I pull in I see a buddy on the pay phone making a drug deal. I hadn't seen him in five years since we graduated from high school. I walked up and said, "Ian what are you doing, man?" He says, "Dave, I've fallen on hard times, I'm living in my car, and things are really messed up right now." I said, "Buddy I don't know if you believe in God, but I believe God had me pull in here, and I believe he had me here to meet you. Can I call you?" He said he didn't have a telephone at this time, so I gave him my number and said, "Please give me a call, I want to help you. I want to share what God's done in my life." We ended up parting on that note because he said he had to get going. He called me a couple weeks later and said a mutual friend of ours, Owen, had shot and killed himself accidentally. Ian was in the apartment, and they were doing drugs, and Owen had accidentally clicked the safety off and then accidentally shot himself; Ian held him as he died. He said it was a wake-up call for him, and he remembered what I told him about the Lord and how God could change his life. He came and lived with me at my house and slept on the couch. He started going to church and gave his life to the Lord.

Question: Will you help me Lord when it's decision time?

Answer:

It was the beginning of my senior year in high school. I was eighteen, and I knew it was big decision time. I needed to get serious about what I wanted to do and where I wanted to go in life. I love drama and the arts but didn't know what I would do with them. Everyone told me that, whatever my choice was, it must be serious. It was my decision to go to Cornish School of the Arts in Seattle. I had a crazy encounter while there with the director of the drama department. He saw me perform and offered me a full ride to Cornish. This was a dream, to be offered a full ride by the board. So attending Cornish became my path my senior year. I went to Christian winter camp in January, and I couldn't get a peace about attending Cornish. God told me, "I know you love to do the arts, Oh how I know you love to do them. Come do what you love to do and then combine that with me and increasing My kingdom." I didn't know how to do that since Cornish is one of the most liberal schools around. Nothing about my plan there was going to be for the kingdom, nothing, and it was all about me. My thinking was all so self-focused. I did not have a peace. So I didn't know why God said, "Find out what you love to do and do it for the kingdom." I had a plan and my teachers were impressed that I was going. I was graduating, and it was just what I was going to do. It was close to the end of my senior year. It was the time of the year when the bios for the yearbook are collected. I was told that I needed to get my final bio in so it could be put with my picture in the yearbook. They asked questions like: What are you going to do? Where are you going? Are you going to Cornish? I just did not have a peace to say, "I'm going to Cornish," so I said, "I'm going to do creative arts for ministry. I don't know what that looks like, I don't know anyone that wants a creative arts planner for their ministry, but that's what I'm going to set out to do." The yearbook staff commented that they thought I was crazy, but that's what they put on my bio. People continued to ask me what my plan was, and I repeated what I had said previously, "I want to work in the creative arts for ministry, somehow, someway." A couple months later I was offered a spot to come on board our school ministry internship program, and it happened to be the first year that they offered a creative arts track. Previously, it had been an internship that was straight ministry, pastoral and the like. They asked if I was interested in creative arts and if so, why don't I come and help. I thought great, creative arts, ministry, it's good. I further thought I would just go to a junior college as well and get my basics out of the way. I wasn't completely happy with it, but I knew it was where God wanted me to be. I did that for the year. Internships were coming to a close, I didn't know where I was going, and I had determined there was nothing more with the school for me in creative arts ministry. There was no job, nothing. I decided to just go to Northwest College and follow that path; that's the easiest thing to do. Six months later, Pastor Dean Curry was voted head pastor of Life Center, my home church in Tacoma, Washington. Pastor Dean contacted me and said he would like to talk to me. I said okay, so we went out to lunch and he said, "I see your giftings. I see you love to do creative arts. I don't know what this is going to look like, and we've never had this position before, but I want you to come on staff and head our creative planning. And you can do what you love to do and do it for the kingdom." He actually used the words that God gave me at winter camp two years prior. I said to myself, this is it; this is what I'm supposed to do. Thankfully I am still at Life Center using the gifting that God gave me obediently for the kingdom. I've learned that I'm not in charge of outcomes; thankfully, I'm not responsible for them; God is. I'm just responsible to be obedient to him. At times I felt like I was giving up a lot through the process, but I have come to realize that I have gained everything and could not be happier. I am thankful for that faith walk that really began at winter camp.

Question: Is God capable of inserting His design even when you are not looking for it?

Answer:

The most significant move or change in my life came in my sophomore year in college at Seattle Pacific University (SPU), a Christian college. The first Free Methodists had created the beginnings of SPU, so they required that all students take certain Bible and theology classes. I was used to that because I had grown up in Christian schools and had taken various Bible classes in all my pre-college schooling. At some point in high school it wasn't that I lost my faith; it just wasn't really alive; it was just "normal." I made my decision to go to SPU based on basketball, not that it was a Christian university, so being at a Christian university was not the determining factor. As a result of my attitude, I wasn't too excited about taking the Bible and theology classes at the time. What I'm saying is the Bible really didn't speak to me; it was kind of dull. My sophomore year I was in the second of the classes—it was actually the year I took Christian scriptures of the Old and New Testaments. It was in the classroom that I felt prompted and directed by God. I was planning on majoring in exercise science and had enrolled in anatomy and physiology and related classes and had no intention of majoring in theology and studying God's word. It was through that class and that professor that God showed up. I didn't know where He was specifically leading; I just knew I was supposed to switch majors. I was to get out of exercise science and switch to theology. That's what I did, not because I had a clear path, but because God had spoken. I knew he had awakened me and that my personal walk with him had begun.

Question: Can God bless a childless couple unexpectivly?

Answer:

In September of 2007 we were contacted by Washington state to see if we were acceptable to have a child at our home so she could get to know her biological family. We did not know anything about her; in fact we didn't even know there was a family member in the foster care system. We found out she was related to us through a nephew, so we said sure. They contacted us about a week and a half later and asked us if we would be interested in considering the adoption of this child. We said we were still startled that we had a family member in the child care system and we needed to pray. Then we began to pray and pray and pray. I told God, "You know the situation with this child. I'm forty-eight and my husband's fifty. If you want her to live with us then open the doors, and we will do what's needed to bring her home." She came to live with us on weekends so she could remain in school in Kitsap County, and we could test the relationship waters. When she finished her school year eight months later, she came to our home full-time. She had come from a very abusive background, and she had been placed in a home for adoption as a baby along with seven other children, and those adoptions had failed traumatically. Parental rights were rescinded, and she was placed up for adoption. In February 2009 we started our six-month waiting period. On June 4 of that year she came to live with us full-time and just a week and a half ago our adoption became permanent. That day was blessed by God from the time we got up that morning to the end of the day. God's hand was in everything including the judge, who had been adopted, and our server at lunch, who was a Christian. We were touched by so many that day. It was just amazing to come home and know that she was ours. Our prayers, because of our age, were for the Lord to give us the strength to keep up with her and the wisdom to care for her. At some point, realizing that God placed her in our home, we knew He's going to give us everything we need for her. There is such a special blessing in this because my husband and I were unable to have children and in fact had given up thinking we could have any children. At our current stage of life we weren't giving any thought toward adopting children. It was just totally God from the time we met Sarah; He made it easy, and we bonded almost immediately. We didn't experience any of those horror stories you hear about or anything close. This little girl is blessed with a great love for Jesus and with everything this little girl has been through in her first ten years God has protected her mind and heart. She is a sweet loving little girl who we will continue raising with His blessing and counsel.

Question: Is this leading the future you have prepared for me?

Answer:

I received a new leading from the Lord earlier this year. I've worked in the family business for thirty-three years, ever since graduating from college. Earlier this year I sensed that the Lord was calling me to a ministry in hospital visitation. I began volunteering at St. Joseph's Medical Center, and they assigned me to the medical physical area even though that is normally a career path for a medical student. I was comfortable with it, and they thought it was a good fit for me. I visited with patients, helped train volunteers, and got to feel familiar in an institution where there's care and compassion for patients. Sometimes there are extreme circumstances with people on the edge of eternity, and I am led to pray for them and support their families. A few months ago, I started transitioning into the pastoral care department, and it was a stretch, but the leading was clear. It has been a growing process, and as I walked from orientation to orientation I often asked myself what I was doing there. I've never had seminary training for this, I don't have the letters following my name that are required for this, but I know within me I am led to do it. The people orientating me assured me that they have no problem with my lack of official qualification, and they didn't see it as an obstacle. It's like I'm passing through a door to a room and another door into another room and on and on, a trusting and growing type of experience. I worked in the state legislature previously, and in fact that was my career direction and education. I have a graduate degree in public administration and worked in the state auditor's office during graduate school. I thought that's where my education would lead me. However, I've discovered at this time in my life that it is my part-time volunteer work that has actually become my dream, fulfillment, and purpose. That's what has been happening to me this year, and it is the most significant thing that has ever happened to me. I did acquire credentials for ministry this year and even had the privilege of performing my daughter's wedding ceremony.

Question: Do I serve a God who cares about the little things?

Answer:

Early November of 2009 we had a cold spell in Washington state. On this morning I woke and began seeking God that I might know what he had in store for me this day. It seemed that every worldly thing was trying to interfere with my drawing near to Him. But the need to meet Him in a significant way was even greater. I lay face down on my living room rug, so things would not interfere with seeking His presence, seeking Him in prayer and praise. And frankly I was well toward achieving that goal and was drawing near to God. All of a sudden I heard in that familiar voice in my head, "hose bib." Not hearing anything else I put it aside and continued seeking God and once again, "hose bib." Finding no reason for this statement, I continued, and again," hose bib." I talked to Him and said the only thing I know to do is to get up, go outside, and look at my hose bib. It was about ten degrees outside, so I slipped on my shoes and jacket and headed outside to look at the hose bib. As I approach my hose bib (outside water faucet), I realized that I had not taken the precaution of disconnecting my hose and insulating the faucet. What I was looking at was a disaster because a large ice ball had formed around the hose/faucet connection. I decided to fill a water bucket with lukewarm water, melt the ice, and remove the hose. The method was successful. I tested the faucet and found it was in good working order. I went to my second outside faucet and repeated this procedure with the same results. Returning inside, praising God for caring about my hose bibs; a potential expensive experience was avoided. He began telling me, "Surely if I care about the hose bibs in your life how much more do I care about the greater things in your life." What a big caring God, one who sees to all our needs and desires, a God who cares about all things small and large.

Question: What is the purpose of life?

Answer:

An instance I felt the Lord speaking very strongly to me, in my spirit, occurred a few months ago. I had been wrestling with the situations and circumstances in my life. A lot of times when I go through life, I ask God, "What is the purpose of this? Why does this need to be a part of my path or my story?" I remember agonizing over it because a lot of times when you go through certain circumstances, you have a pre-planned outcome. You have this idealized outcome that you think it is supposed to be, or what you want it to be, while all the time God is just asking you to trust Him through the circumstance. Even though I wanted to know the purpose "right now," I felt He was saying to me, "If you really want to figure out life's purposes or the purpose of this situation, you have to be okay with the outcome. You can't just be okay with the outcome you have in your mind; that may not even be my purpose. It's a matter of trusting Me through it and trusting the outcome will be good and that My purposes are good."

Wow, we ask God for an answer, then go about giving Him the design or outcome we think is proper or right. Ask yourself what's that all about? My prayer is: "When you answer, Lord, I will listen. Where you lead Lord, I will follow. That is the obedience I want in my life and I will speak it in faith and it will be."

Question: Am I valuable?

Answer:

The summer between ninth and tenth grade I went to camp near Lake Chelan in eastern Washington. I was living a very unhappy life. I mean, I was so unhappy I thought life sucked; I thought I'd never be anybody or anything. Some of my buddies had gone to this camp, and I remember being on the bus thinking I don't want to be here while at the same time going through withdrawals from tobacco. I was angry and cranky and thinking I really didn't know anyone here. After getting there, accompanied with myself and my bad attitude, we had a meeting that had worship and the message. Before going to the meeting, I had no expectation, but the speaker said something that impacted me in an amazing way:he said you are very valuable to God not unlike a precious plate that's been stored in a china cabinet and been removed and broken. The Holy Spirit took what now seems like a funny little comparison and began an incredible change in my life. Something inside me just broke. The idea that God would consider me valuable and even precious blew my mind. I remember going from tears of joy and ultimately feeling renewed and clean inside. At that time in my life I had two sets of friends, my rebel friends and my friends who encouraged me to go to Bible study and be accountable. I had grown up in a Christian home but kept one foot in the world. After that experience I tipped toward my Christian friends, and since that time I have been able to get that foot that was in the world to work toward the path Jesus has designed for me.

Question: Is it possible that an ounce of obedience can produce a pound of cure?

Answer:

My wife and I walked into a tanning salon. She was going to tan for twenty minutes before we went shopping. I was seated in the waiting area, and the girl working the front was holding her head. I said to her, "Are you okay? You look like you're in pain." She said, "Oh, I'm having a migraine headache. I take shots every couple weeks, and it is just bad right now." I said, "I don't want you to think I'm a strange person, but I'm a Jesus person and I would really like to pray for you right now. I have seen Jesus heal AIDS and seen him heal cancer. I believe in God's power, and I believe Jesus can heal you. Would you mind if I pray for you? There have been times when I have prayed for people and they did not get healed so I'm not guaranteeing you healing, but I'd just like to pray." She agreed, and I prayed a very simple prayer like, "I just ask in the name of Jesus that these headaches be healed; I know you are able Lord; amen. My wife came out, the receptionists thanked me, and we left. I came back about two weeks later and the receptionist said, "Hey you're the prayer guy." I said, "Oh yes I prayed for you." She said, "Since that day you walked out my headache went away, and I have not had the slightest headache since. I've had them every day the past five years. I think you're God healed me." At that point I got to share the gospel with her and told her just how she could invite Jesus into her heart. We did not have a lot of time together because she was busy with customers, and I did not want to embarrass her. I do believe that God provided just the right amount of time to love and heal.

Question: Was it nothing but the truth that saved me?

Answer:

The biggest leading God ever gave me in my life was when he first came to me. It was a wedding where I was invited to be a groomsman. About nine months before I was invited to be the groomsman, I was involved in a drug deal where I lost $180,000 and beat the bullets out the door. Until then I had been an extremely high level drug dealer, the average drug deal being in the hundreds of thousands of dollars. I had a really successful entertainment company with a record label and a magazine, and I was promoting two clubs in Seattle. I was living a life of what seemed like immortality at the time. This was all masked in a childhood that was extremely abusive; I grew up a biker kid with a hippie mom. When my deal went bad, I went home and prayed to a God that I did not know yet. I said, "If this is not the life you want me to live, show me the one you want." Something happened that day. It wasn't like it happened overnight, but that day I got real curious, not only because of the near-death experience but I had also been told that day my girlfriend was three-and-one-half months pregnant with my baby boy. Eight months into the pregnancy the Drug Enforcement Administration came knocking on my door with a federal indictment. The prosecutor was giving me thirty-five days to come in and talk to him, or I was going to be federally indicted by a grand jury. That is during the time I got invited to be a groomsman at my buddy's wedding. Mark, the groom, had been saved for two years and since that time had always talked about Jesus Christ. I must mention that Mark had also been my right-hand man. Mark went to his pastor and asked who he should have as its groomsman because there were his best friends on the other side of the fence, and there were his new Christian brothers. Bob said pick two and two. Pick two Christian brothers and two guys from the past that you want to see saved. I was one of the guys he picked. At that wedding when Harry, Mark's father-in-law, began talking about Jesus Christ it was like the first glass of water I drank, and it was cold, clear and clean. It made me more curious, and then he said four words that changed my life forever," Isn't the Lord good?" There was something about the way he said it, and I knew that these guys had responded. There was just something about these guys responding to this Lord that I wanted to know more about. The groomsman's gift was *The 40 Days of Purpose* by Rick Warren. I took it home and read it, and without consciously realizing it, I had submitted that day. The reason I know it is when I left that wedding I was so struck by Christ's love for us and the wedding party's love for Christ that I was changed on my way home. I walked into that building feeling one way, and I walked out feeling totally different. I couldn't listen to the same music, I couldn't look at women the same, and I couldn't have the same friends. I just knew my life was going to be different after that day. On the day in the *40 Days* book when it asks if you want to give your life to Christ right now, here is how you do it, I think I was baptized in the Holy Spirit. Every day since that day has been a revelation from Christ, and every day has been living for Him. As a result of my indictment I was supposed to get ten years to life, so I got a really high priced attorney who got my sentence knocked down to three years in prison. We walked into the courtroom, and the deal was made between my attorney and a federal prosecutor. After looking at the deal, the judge turned to me and said I don't know who the real Jeff Fisher is; on the one hand you have this criminal record since you were a kid and started in drugs when you were in your single digits. On the other hand you always have been inventive and made lots of money, so I want to know who the real Jeff Fisher is. Why don't you get up on the stand and tell me. I got up there and my lawyer had prepared this letter with everything I was supposed to say when I got on the stand. You know, like I'm sorry for the things I have done and so on and so on. However when I got there I just started crying because of the weight of the situation. My baby son was now six months old; a potential prison sentence and it all was just crushing me. I was crying so I couldn't even read the paper. I just spoke and said if I knew back then what I had to lose now I would have never done any of that stuff. But back then I didn't have anything to lose, back then I had nothing. I said if I had the offer to change diapers now I would; most of my friends think that's a really a funny thing. I know Jesus Christ now, and I've got a real role model. I've got new friends, a whole new city, and a new life. So that's who I am. The judge sat totally silent for like two minutes, and it seemed like forever. He said, "I believe you have a shot. Most guys in your position don't have a chance, but I'm going to give you a shot. I'm going to give you six months of home arrest and three years of probation. I advise you, you have seen the lighter side of my nature, but my nature has another side, and if I ever see you again you'll experience that." I knew what had just happened because my partner had just been sentenced to 120 months. So I was spared that day.

Question: Does confirmation come from other people?

Answer:

I was in a marriage for quite a while that was very unhealthy. I knew in my spirit there was something not right but couldn't quite put my finger on it. I cried out to the Lord, sought counseling, and had a woman in my life who told me, "Heather, you just need to pray for the truth; the truth will set you free." I went before God and said, "God, I give this marriage to you. I need the truth and whatever the truth is, I will accept it." When I prayed it was as if a weight was lifted, and I just waited on the answer. Soon, just over the course of a few days, the most a week, the truth was shed on activities that were going on behind my back. The truth caused fear, but I approached and confronted my husband and I told him I was willing to work on our marriage and suggested we seek counsel or whatever it takes. But he was unwilling. The situation scared me because here I was with two little girls and an unknown future. It was a very frightening time. However, at the same time I faced these fears, there was peace in me that spoke of a God that was bigger than my circumstance. And I know that I couldn't have made it through that period alone. How else could I wake up every morning and face the day and make decisions that had to be made, joyfully. How would I face the challenges of going back to school, finding a home, providing for my two girls and myself? That fact that I'm standing up on these two feet is only possible because of Jesus. At times when I financially did not know how I would make it, I would go to my checkbook and make deductions, and somehow there would be money left over. I thought, "That is not the way it happens in the real world," but with God as my provider, it does. It's just amazing. I liken those days as though I were walking through a dark tunnel, and yet there was always light at the end, and that light was Jesus. He was faithful beyond measure. A card would show up at just the right time; an encouraging phone call or word of encouragement would come my way. One of my prayers is, "Lord, please make it clear so I can understand, so that I can make the right decisions, so that I know this is your plan for my life." One of my core beliefs is that we commonly receive confirmation by way of other humans, to answer the needs in our lives. And often I am able to say, "Yes! That's truly from God." I have those moments of loneliness, but at the same time I'm believing and knowing God is faithful and will see to my needs as I remain faithful to Him. There is a woman, who is just an acquaintance at church, who came up to me with tears in her eyes and said, "The Lord put you on my heart last week, and I have been praying for you. He told me to tell you that He sees your faithfulness and knows your heart, and He has a plan for you." This was overwhelming. I just started crying and said, "You don't even know how much that means to me." The timing was perfect because I had been praying privately, "Lord, I'm faithful; do you see my broken heart?" Of course He did, and He told a woman to pray and later to come give me this word of confirmation and comfort. His answer and her obedience became a hug from Jesus to me.

SECTION THREE: DREAMS AND VISIONS

This subject can be controversial—if not weighed in with certain truths. God has used dreams and visions throughout biblical history to inform, encourage, warn, guide, direct, and correct man. One of the first God-inspired dreams mentioned is in Genesis 20:3 given to Abimelech. God further spoke in dreams and visions to many others including, Jacob, Joseph, Abraham, Solomon, King Nebuchadnezzar, Daniel, King David, and the apostles Peter and Paul.

In Acts 2:16–18, the apostle Luke writes of Peter's words in reference to the final days. Verses 17 and 18 state: "But this is that which was spoken by the prophet Joel; And it shall come to pass in the last days, saith God, I will pour out of my Spirit upon all flesh: and your sons and daughters shall prophesy and your young sons shall see visions, and your old men shall dream dreams."

Is it not now the last days spoken of here in Acts?

Question: Who am I and do I serve any good purpose?

Answer:

For many years I did not trust God's grace was sufficient to cover a guy like me. There was really no chance I could serve God in the fullness which he wanted me to. Not worthy to represent him, often going to bed tossing and turning, berating myself and generally not liking myself at all. For short periods I was able to accept the forgiveness of God he so readily gives but not able to hold on to it. My wife would often remind me that I was not God and that a sinless life was not possible, but forgiveness was mine. Looking back, this self-abuse was just an excuse, in a way, for not serving Him in a greater way. Fear, ego, pride, and all sorts of the human fleshly types of thinking were not of Him but me. It got so ridiculous at times that I would condemn myself for condemning myself. Knowing that this thinking was totally of the enemy I began seeking, in earnest prayer, a solution from God. God had an answer.

One night after going through this self-abuse process once again, I fell asleep and began to dream. In this dream there was a large party being held for me; everyone I knew my whole life was there. They were all standing around in little groups sharing with each other. The subject matter of their conversations was all of the errors or mistakes that Ralph had made in his life. They were not speaking mean-spirited; they were just stating facts about me. Now I was doing my best to be a good host, but as you must know it was not uplifting. In order to remain an even-tempered, well-mannered host, I determined a short drive was in order. I found myself driving down the woodsy lane thinking about the party and what had happened. Because I was not paying attention to my driving, the truck slid off the road and ended up in the ditch. Getting out and observing the damage, I began to use the old self-abuse language. In the distance a vehicle was approaching, an old vehicle with suicide doors, and just as I observed it, a woman, came tumbling out the rear door, apparently thrown out. The vehicle sped off. Putting aside my concerns, I ran to her aid and while doing so observed a funny looking guy on a knoll behind her. It appeared he had a fireball in the hand and was about to throw it at her. Viewing this as a danger, I grabbed her just in time to avoid the fiery missile. Not knowing who I was or what my intentions were, she pulled away and began to run. By this time the funny looking guy had loaded up with another fireball, had thrown it, and hit her directly. Immediately I was transported to the forest and was sitting on a chair in front of a great stage. There were beautiful ballerinas performing on the stage. It was a beautiful serene setting—the forest, the stage, and the dancers. Suddenly I recognized that one of the dancers was the lady who had been thrown from the car. Her life story was revealed to me. I knew that she had always wanted to be a dancer, but her thinking was that she wasn't good enough, or she didn't have the time and continually made statements to herself discouraging herself from achieving this end. I realized the funny looking man with the fireball had not been an enemy, but friend, a man who threw encouragement and love in people's lives so that they might take the chance to be the best they could be. This was God's design for him. I thought maybe this guy could help me. Just as I thought that, I realized that this fellow was seated next to me and that his name was "Gwedo." I turned to ask if he could help me, and he immediately responded in the affirmative and stood and began to wrap his arms around me. While he was doing, this we became one, and I realized that I was this Gwedo. God had designed me to throw fireballs of His encouragement, knowledge, and wisdom into people's lives and that in fact had been doing so for many years. I remember thinking this Gwedo is all right. He is part of the cure, not the problem. What a new awareness had been given me. I was a good guy with God's purposes in mind. That was the first time I was able to forgive my shortcomings and receive what God had made me.

I awoke, got up and wrote this entire dream experience down so that I could share it with my wife in the morning. The next morning my wife and I were having coffee and I slid the story in front of her and asked if she would read it and respond. She read it, got up, and began doing dishes. I sat silently as long as I could last and then began probing her for some meaningful response. Her first response was, "You miss-spelled Gwedo; its spelled Guido." I laughed and said, "Well honey I never was much of speller." I want you to know that I believe this was a message from God for me, and furthermore I feel heaviness has lifted off of me. With that she chose to agree with me, not too enthusiastically, but agreed. I got up and kissed her and left for work. My office was approximately thirty to forty minutes driving time from my home, and it was my practice to pray, plan, and organize my day during this drive. I had done so and was about six or eight blocks from work when that voice, that inner voice of God said to me clearly, "By the way you didn't spell Gwedo wrong, it means Gee-We-Do. It means that if you will remain in me we can do anything." What an amazing message from a God who loves me, who cared enough to communicate with me in a manner on a level that I could accept and understand. He gave me a new name and a new way of looking at myself.

God has been speaking to me about that dream I had some fifteen-plus years ago and reminding me of its use for the Kingdom. It seemed that each time I shared this identity I was once again encouraged and empowered to serve Him. It gave others courage to seek God for their identity. God had named me a valuable person useful to His plan and purpose. One day, just a few weeks ago while praying and reflecting on how thankful I was that God would speak to me, the Spirit prompted me to look up the meaning of the name "Guido." Strange, I thought, after all the years, but I knew it was God directing me. I went to my computer and first typed in my spelling, "Gwedo," and found nothing. Next I typed in "Guido" and found there are two meanings:

The Germanic—Forest

The Italian—Guide

God began speaking to me that the dreams and visions and communications through His word and prayer He had given me far exceeded any other form of study or self-learning I could ever have. He told me that they were for His purposes, and it is blindness and fear and lack of obedience that has kept them silent in us. I have determined, because I know all He said is true, that I must at every opportunity share these communications with others. They were not given just for me but for the building of the Kingdom.

This dream has opened many doors to people's hearts. It has given me a platform to introduce a Savior, Lord, and God to some who may have never known him. The telling of this love story has set me and other captives free, and it can subdue and eliminate the lying attacks of Satin. Jesus has given you an equally important story; share it.

Question: Can visions lead to ministry?

Answer:

I was thirty-five and had a vision that was not like an out-of-body experience. This vision occurred in the Michael W. Smith concert about eighteen years ago. There was this guitar player on stage; his name was something like Steve E., and he was just rocking out, and something about that just moved me. I turned to my friend Stephen and said, "Someday I'm going to play like that, I just have to." At that time I didn't know how to play the guitar, but it just grabbed me suddenly and compelled me to learn to play. Now I play at church a couple times a week, and it is the most fulfilling thing to me because I feel it is an offering to the Lord. I can strive to be excellent in something I enjoy and give it to the Lord as part of my worship and praise for him.

Question: Am I responsible for that?

Answer:

I had a dream, and in this dream I saw a big scroll. I could see a timeline on the scroll that went back to the beginning when God created the earth and then into our future. All the nations and leaders were listed on the scroll as if all the people of the earth were moving forward. What I noticed was there were great leaders, good and bad, on the list, making things happen. Those that were involved in the flow were like lights on the scroll. Those leaders that were not involved, who just sat watching things happen both good and bad, were dark. Those that were trying to make something happen for the Lord were like lights and were helping carry the flow of what God was doing forward. As I looked at this, it seemed a great amount people were sitting on the sidelines, and I decided I wanted to be one of those lights in the middle of the flow, and I did not want to be one of those dark ones on the sidelines. At the time of the dream I was the children's pastor at a large church, and I did not concern myself with anything outside of the children's ministry. The rest of the church was not important; I just wanted to do my own thing. I saw things in the church that needed to be done, but I thought, that's not my job, but when I woke up from that dream I came to a new realization: I'm responsible for what happens here. I can't just run a department here; I'm not just a part of the periphery here. I'm a leader here and if I see that God wants to do something in the church I AM responsible. So, this new thinking was a huge shift for me; I was doing a task and doing it well but not worrying about the rest of the church. My new position was, as long as I am here, I am responsible to do what God wants done, and if I do nothing when I see it, it may not get done. So I made a shift, and part of that new thinking is what spawned the children's outreach in the community and the development of connect groups within our church.

Question: Why am I telling the things I have tried to conceal?

Answer:

My husband and I both had the Holy Spirit leading to join the church we had been attending. We joined the alpha class and there was an adult weekend coming up I wanted to attend. The more classes and services I attended gave me a feeling that I had a place in this church; I actually belong here. I had just had a vision as I was sitting in church listening to pastor on stage. I viewed myself sitting up on stage, for whatever reason, next to pastor. It didn't seem I was really saying anything, but I felt right at home. It was just a brief but very real vision as I sat there. My husband and I got into the car after church to go home, and my husband said to me that he felt I was going to be up on that stage one day. I laughed at him and said, "That's funny because when I was in church I saw myself sitting up there with pastor on the stage." As a result of God's plan, the next week I was on the stage telling thousands of people the facts I had tried to put behind me about my past. I always thought that people didn't want to know the garbage I had walked through. I went up there and told everybody about how I'd been in prison, how I'd lost my kids, about my life in drugs, and how Jesus had delivered me out of it completely. There I was up on stage telling these people what I had been trying so hard to keep from them.

Question: Is this real? Is this me? Is this you Lord?

Answer:

I've always known that I was called of God into ministry. Being born into a pastor's home, my heart as a young teen was turned toward the Lord, and at night as I lay in bed, tears would roll down onto my pillow. I gave my life over to God into whatever calling he would have me do. For some reason that was so important. I didn't know then specifically what my life would look like, perhaps a pastor's wife or full-time ministry. It was very important to me to make a difference in life however He chose. I began teaching Sunday school when I was twelve and began throwing my heart into whatever little ministry God gave me to serve. It became the delight of my life to serve Him. It was just so amazing. Later as opportunities grew and as I got married and had children, I came to a point where the opportunities became more big-time. They were more about adult teachings, more callings out of my comfort zone. I was resistant but doing a lot of volunteer work in women's ministry and a variety of other ministry. Beyond that I felt I was being called into another level. It didn't frighten me, but I felt inadequate, and so I was praying and wrangling in my spirit, wondering just how God was going to use me in my inadequacy. I went to bed one night and had been desperately praying during this period of time about going to this new level. I had a dream that I was speaking at a podium, which wasn't particularly unusual at this time in my life. God anointed me with oil and I felt that oil flow from the top of my head down through my hair, neck, and onto my shoulders. I felt so anointed and so wrapped in his Holy Spirit. I looked around to see if anyone else noticed, but they didn't; they just appeared to be listening. Then I gave an altar call, and the altars were full; people responded. I woke up with that anointing, just the feel of that oil on me as if it were real. I laid and pondered. Is this real? Is this me? Is this you Lord? I took His hand and trusted him and went on teaching and speaking into leadership as he led. Thinking back, He equips each step of the way, and the Holy Spirit empowers. He takes your hand and goes before you, and that's exactly what has happened. This anointing over the years has developed in ways and areas that I could not have dreamed. He's taking me down roads that I could never have anticipated. It's His anointing and His calling, and all I need to do is trust Him.

Question: Is there anything that is bad, that God cannot change for good?

Answer:

In about January of 2007, I had a vision I was lying in bed, and two bright lights came on both sides of me. I sat up, trying to determine what was happening to me, and just as I was trying to figure it out, I was taken up in the air with these two bright lights on both sides of me. We were flying over a familiar area to me in Shelton, Washington, and I saw ahead a casino called the Little Creek Casino. I saw the facility itself and the signage I had seen for many years. As we were flying by the sign, it did not say Little Creek Casino, like normal, but instead it said, International Miracle Center. After that we started going into the casino but viewing it from above, ceiling to floor. Knowing the layout quite well because I go there and pray frequently, I could not help noticing it was completely changed inside. What I saw were various segments of the casino working in a completely different way. Inside where there had been a smoke-free gambling area, there instead was a large group of people, an intercessory type gathering, praying, and worshiping along with little kids dancing with the music. We went to the next room where there had been a buffet and instead was a series of healing rooms, one after another. Hurting people lined up waiting to be prayed for in the healing rooms. The next room, instead of being a large gambling room as the location of all the casino slot machines and tables, was now a large open gathering room. This room was filled wall-to-wall with hundreds of chairs facing a stage area. I was viewing the room from the back with a ground-level perspective. I said to the lights that remained with me, "It's kind of strange, just a bunch of empty chairs." Then a voice from the light said, "No, look closer." I looked closer, and I could see all the people were on their faces, on the floor, in front of their chairs, and I could also see an awesome black and gray cloud which hung over the entire building. I was told the glory of the Lord was in the house with the power and presence of God. I looked to the stage and the whole worship group was on their faces before God, and there was just an awesome presence of God everywhere. We moved next to the dining area, and it was the same as before and continued from there to the hotel. The voice from the light said, "The hotel is going to be used to bring in terminally ill from all over the world. They will be flown to the local airport just down the road and transported to this place. The hotel will house these patients, and the teams from the healing rooms will come through twenty-four hours a day and pray with the sick, and they will be sent back home after being totally healed. I observed a constant flow of people involved in trainings and ministry. All of a sudden it hit me: I'm seeing a futuristic view of what this vision is all about; it's a complete ministry operation. I was just in awe, not only to see this operation, but I was being trained by these lights, which I presume were angels, a conclusion I'm very comfortable with. They were not only instructing me on how to manage this future facility but how to lay it out properly. I was told this would be the first of many like it. That tribe after tribe, casino after casino, would no longer be operating as casinos but would be large training and healing centers equipping the people in all areas of ministry. People would be coming to these locations because there would not be the doctors or hospitals available and affordable. They would have these healing communities on tribal grounds where they could be safe and free. People would be coming from all around the world to work in, be trained in, and experience the miracles of God. I woke up with just in a state of exhaustion yet elation from the download that I was given. I woke up my wife and told her I had just been in the most amazing place.

Question: How much of me do you want Lord?

Answer:

During my life and growth, when I was learning about the Lord, I became a regular evangelist. I was led to share the gospel with people that had been like me, religious, but really did not know the Lord. I discovered through a dream what God wanted for me.

In my dream I woke up in the morning and went out on the deck and smelled honeysuckle in the air; it was just beautiful. It reminded me of a wonderful experience I had with a friend who was now living by a lake in a brand-new home. I wanted to see her, so I asked my son, who was in junior high and living at home at the time, if he wanted to go with me and visit my friend. He agreed, and as we approached her home, we could see that there were a lot of new homes there and that her home sat about the length of a football field away from the lake. We went inside; it was so new and beautiful, and she had provided refreshments and was a great hostess. All of a sudden we heard a siren from an emergency vehicle. We opened the door and observed that a lot of people were gathered down by the lake along with the rescue crew. We decided we would walk down and see for ourselves just what was up. I looked around for my son to invite him along, but he was not there. The next door neighbor was looking out at the crowd from her upstairs window. I asked if she could see what was happening, and she said it appeared that someone had drowned. We continued on down, and the circle of people was so tightly grouped that I could not get in to see what was happening, but my friend did. For about four or five minutes I could hear the rescue squad working very hard, and yet the people around them were very silent. It was so quiet I could hear the gentle lapping of the waves at the shore, but I could see nothing. After about thirty minutes, I was able to see one of the rescue men. He stood up, looked right in my eyes, and asked, "Have we done enough?" I continued watching and the next thing I knew the emergency people were loading their equipment into their trucks, and the crowd disappeared as if they had never been there. I stood there and looked at this sheet-covered body and became curious enough to see who was under the sheet. I lifted up the corner, and I was looking into the face of my son; I knew enough had not been done. I just started to call the emergency people back, and I woke up from the dream. As I woke I thought, "I've got to do something; there is something abnormal about this dream." All that day I wondered what significance this dream might have in my life, what it meant. Later, God began to interpret. The rescue crew represented the preachers, teachers, and evangelists who go out and try to share the gospel message with those people who are dead and in need of rescue. The crowd I could not penetrate was the people who were contented in church to just sit there and let the preachers and teachers and evangelists do everything. The fact that I could not get through the crowd was Jesus calling me out of the crowd to get involved. He showed me when I looked into the eyes of my son just a glimpse of what He feels when people die and they don't know him. It was my love for my son that showed me how important it was to talk to people about Jesus. From that point on, after the dream, things started happening in my life, and I was called by my pastor to get involved with a second wave of a program called evangelistic explosion. It was a teaching that was occurring at the Lutheran church we attended. I didn't really want to get involved, but after that dream I agreed, and that was the first training I got involved with. The first people I witnessed to after the training were a man and a woman who had been attending the Lutheran church, and I shared my testimony. The man was not receptive, but the woman was, and I wondered to myself that he would not make it if he died today. In a short period of time we began going to an Assembly of God (AG) Church. We had become a little discouraged with the Lutheran Church because people came and they did not return, and we felt that the ministry was not alive enough. The first person I met in the library of the new church was the man I had witnessed to at the other church. I said, "I can't believe it. What are you doing here?" He said he had grown up in AG churches and that my testimony had gotten him to come back to his church. He's now been on the evangelism trail ever since and plays the piano in several churches each Sunday. He loves the Lord and shares the gospel freely. That dream and the gospel are now ingrained in me, and I will continue sharing it.

Question: I wonder; should I create some ripples?

Answer:

At nineteen years of age, I was at a Christian camp leading worship, and afterwards there was a prayer time. A gentleman came up to me and said that God had put an impression on his heart that I would be doing this worship ministry for a long time. He went on to explain that God had given him a vision of a rock dropping into a lake and the ripples going out, representing what my ministry would look like. It was not just a thing that I'm good at music or enjoy music but that my music was going to touch people. Prior to the time the man had spoken to me I had been praying about what God would have for me. What is my purpose? What am I supposed to be doing? During this questioning period I had the same vision of rock in water, ripples going out, but was not given a context. Ever since that day it has been solidified in me that the knowledge and desire that what I was created to be was not just a fun hobby. I honestly feel that music ministry is what I was created for, and that I was created to lead worship. That moment is extremely vivid in my mind. I remember everything about it still—the colors, the smell, the taste—and that's probably the most important thing God has ever given to me.

Question: What can I do with the gifts and talents you have given me Lord?

Answer:

God spoke to me through a dream. In this dream I saw myself standing in front of the congregation preaching. I had just been ordained a couple of weeks prior and was ordained in an entirely African-American church. In this dream I was speaking to a congregation which was made up of all caucasian people. This was very out of my comfort zone. I woke up thinking, "Wow! That was a heck of a

dream." I was living in Phoenix, Arizona, at the time and I was thinking, well this place must be somewhere like in Montana because that's
the only community I can think of with an all-white population. Three
years later when God closed every door possible for me to find work
in Arizona and sent me and my family to a place we knew nothing
about in Bellingham, Washington, I knew an adventure was at hand.
In 1990 in Bellingham I was soon to learn that there were only 150
black people in a community of 190,000 people. So God moved us
and I began working for the city of Bellingham.

Working for Bellingham was not a completely fulfilling job because
I had a passionate desire to minister to the body of Christ. I knew God
had given me gifts to do that, but I was always doing it as a hobby and
not as a career. Ministry was a nonpaying job I enjoyed, and I served as
an assistant pastor at different churches, helping to organize ministries,
always working with someone else's vision. I was sitting in my office in
city hall, and I said, "God I just can't do this anymore." Within a week
of saying that, God moved me in the spirit and I was out of that job
and looking. Within two weeks of leaving that job, a pastor friend of
mine hired me. Before I was hired by the pastor, I was speaking to God
in a prayer time and I said, "God I know you have given me gifts, and
the word says, 'I will make room for your gifts.'" At that time, the Holy
Spirit just spoke to me and said, Felix, this is my game, and right now
I have you sitting on the bench. I don't want you to fall asleep on the
bench; I want you to pay attention to the game. When I turn to you or
point to you, I want you to get up and get in the game, as if you had been

in the game the entire time. This is where I have you now, but this is not where you will always be." So he gave me an assurance He had a plan a place and a purpose for me.

Question: I don't feel you; are you there, God?

Answer:

The first thing that comes to my mind is a vision, really an experience that God gave me. My husband and I were in the transition of his becoming the head pastor of Life Center in Tacoma, Washington. God had given him dreams as a young kid, then as a young man, then as a young adult, not just leading but actual dreams, and in them God revealed that he would be the head pastor at Life Center one day. When we got together, we based our lives on following that leading and knowing those dreams. We had grown in leadership at Life Center for eighteen years when pastor Buntain announced his upcoming retirement. We knew that God had called us to Life Center but journeyed through a year or longer of the church board looking at other options. That was a tough year for us, very tough, excruciating, because we knew that God had called us, yet it seemed so far in the opposite direction that we kind of wondered, where is God? And at one point it looked pretty much impossible. There were so many things that had to happen for God to fulfill that dream. On the human side it was honestly impossible. I remember at an extremely low moment I cried out to God questioning what was happening but at the same time trusting Him. I remembered saying to God, "I feel like you've left; I don't get this." One of my passions is running, and I was running through Point Defiance Park on trails by myself. As I ran I was calling out to the Lord saying, "I feel alone, and I feel like You've left, and I don't understand where You are, and why You haven't come through." At that moment God spoke to me: "I am here." That's all He said. I kept running and began using my prayer language thanking him for that word to me because I knew it was so obviously Him. I had a peace come over me, I finished my run and ended up in an open field, and I questioned the Lord again saying, "I know you hear Lord but I still feel abandoned." At that time some birds came close to me and began flying circles around me about five feet from my head and the Lord spoke to me and said, "I'm surrounding you, I'm surrounding you, you're in My sight." It was so strange. The birds just kept flying around my head, so I said, "God okay, I will just keep trusting you." God confirmed through this experience that He was always near regardless of what my feelings might be. He built my faith and proved to me that on the human level things can be impossible but on the God level nothing's impossible.

Question: Can direction from God be just fact and not emotion?

Answer:

The first real defining moment of hearing from the Lord came when I was seventeen years old and at Bible camp. I was in my senior year in high school and attending a camp at Cedar Springs. Ray Larson, who at the time was a pastor from California, was the guest speaker. Ray was preaching one night, and I was sitting in the service between John my best friend and future brother-in-law and my future wife who at the time was my girlfriend. At some point during his message Ray paused and began to talk about the supernatural. At that moment I had a vision of myself up in front of the people preaching. This was a new thought for me because I'm a first-generation Christian, I didn't have any ministry background, and I did not even know what that meant. It was just instantaneous, like you have this vision, that's what you're doing, and it happens, and it's gone. In my spirit, which by the way I've found is the way the Lord works in me often, there was no doubt that it was Him. I always told people if you have real doubt whether it's Him just assume it's not. In my experience I've had dreams of things that I could find meaning in, but this isn't about finding meaning in something this is about it having meaning. The vision is the meaning. I have never had to stretch to figure it out if it was the Lord. This vision I knew was the Lord and I knew the point was that I was going to serve Him in full-time ministry. No sooner did I have this vision than Ray stopped and said, "Someone, right now, had a vision, and you are supposed to be in full-time ministry. I want you to come up here right now." So you know we can process 60,000 thoughts a second in our brain, and it is operating a lot faster than your mouth is operating. We see things, we are taking in information so quickly and instantaneously-you can kind of do the math. I'm seventeen going on eighteen, and if I don't go up there right now I'm going to spend the next seventy years running away from this thing and trying to explain away this moment. I stood up, which was kind of a scary thing to do because I had my buddy on one side and my girlfriend on the other. I went down there, and it wasn't an emotional thing, and I wasn't crying; I didn't even know what I was getting into at that time. I had thought in the past that I would go into business; in fact John and I had talked about going to school together at Western Washington University. But I went forward, and they laid hands on me and prayed for me, and I sat back down. John said, "I guess we're not going to school together." I said, "I guess not." After that my girlfriend said to me," I always wanted to be a pastor's wife," and I said, "Cool."

Question: Will the Holy Spirit have priority over my dieection?

Answer:

I was in India ministering in 2010, and the Saturday night before I brought my last message, I had a dream. We had left on a Tuesday and were returning the following Tuesday, so it was quite a quick trip. I was accompanied by a medical team. While the medical team was using their gifts and abilities, I was doing a conference at a church with the pastors of the English church. The conference started Thursday night, and there were eight other language groups. I did thirteen talks from Thursday to through Sunday. By the time you have done ten presentations, you have said a lot, and the Holy Spirit gives you a connection to the people. When I went to bed Saturday night, I felt like I knew these people, and Sunday was going to be great. I already had in mind what I was going to speak about in the morning and what I was going to speak about the final talk that night. I had a dream that Saturday night, and in the dream I'm in the home of a friend or someone I obviously care about. It was very comfortable. It was as if you and I were having dinner; it was not a new introduction. We could say anything to each other, and there was a sense there was nothing we would not say. We were laughing, and there was warm regard in the room. As I'm sitting in the room, my friend reached into a closet to pull something out, and when he pulled out his arm, a huge, thick snake was wrapped around it. I saw it first and it startled me and I alerted him. He stepped back, and grabbed it by the head and tail. We both felt a sense of relief; he had the thing in his hands so it couldn't bite him or me. We were looking at it thinking, "Wow, how did that thing get in here, and aren't we blessed that it didn't bite someone or get the kids?" We were just generally talking about it while he was holding this thing, and we said a collective praise the Lord. He was holding this thing and went to set it down on the floor. I stopped him and said, "What are you doing? He told me it didn't get us and "I can't hold it all day so I was getting rid of it." I said, "You have got to get it out of the house because as long as it's in the house, it's going to get you or your kids." He said, "Oh yeah." We went over to the door and he threw it out. I woke up from my dream and had the distinct impression that this was a word for the church in Calcutta. Outside the church we were in there was a makeshift temple for their big festival. One of our guys, who had been in the temple, said there was a huge idol shaped like a snake inside. I love the imagery that the Lord gave me in that dream, that the enemy is in the house, and you catch him before he takes you or takes your kids. But then quite often we just casually let him go in the house. So the last talk I told them the story, and I said that I think some of you got out of Hinduism or Islam or whatever and then you proceeded to let it loose in the house again. I said, "I caution you to be careful with that because I think it's a temptation in Calcutta because it's a hyper religious environment." I further think that's it's a temptation here in America because we're in hyper-sensual environment where we get the snake by the head and click back on pornography or ego or start feeding other appetites. This dream sobered me, and I felt like it was for that church and generally for all men.

Question: Are you refining me for a greater purpose?

Answer:

At age twenty-six, God gave me a vision that my role was not leading souls to Christ but was also equipping and unleashing those souls that already believe in Him. He showed me that everything that I had experienced, like the feeling that I've left so much on the table that I did not maximize, He would provide opportunity and His will would be done. The opportunities that He provided for me in the National Football

League (NFL) that I had failed at, He would use to grow the Kingdom. This was a time when He spoke to me through a woman in my life named Mother Sarah Turner. She came to me one day and told me the Spirit of God had told her to confirm with me that I was made after God's own heart. This was a gift that has carried me through many difficult times. God has shown me and continues to show me He is using every experience to grow both me and the Kingdom. He has allowed me to get deeply engaged in the business world for the purpose of taking all those real life happenings and looking at them through the filter of God's word and extrapolating from them the things that are going to build favor for the Kingdom of God. He has shown me that I have only experienced a small glimpse so far as to what He desires to accomplish in me.

SECTION FOUR:
THE VOICE OF GOD

T o begin this fourth section, I will share a bone of mine that became a teaching that the Lord not only has used in redirecting my thinking, but I have used to illustrate as a method of recovery for various addictive problems and the general problem of being able to thrive in the middle of disaster.

A brief history of my working life would be that I was always inclined to be an entrepreneur, successfully owning and running small businesses. I took an early retirement from law-enforcement in 1981 to concentrate on one of those businesses. I purchased a restaurant, which was a leading that God had designed for my life for His purposes. From 1981 to 1987 we will refer to this time period as the, "days of plenty." There was an abundance of money, great ministry, blessing, blessing, blessing, and faithful employees. Between 1987 and 1990 were the "days of plague and famine." The business drops, money goes, attitudes slump, and business fails. Yet, a truth remained in me that God never changes: circumstances yes, God no. If this change was caused by errors in me, they must be identified and corrected. It was certain that my management skills did have room for improvement, but the turnaround was so dramatic that it seemed like a plan. My wife and I had prayed and prayed for guidance after which it was determined that closing the restaurant was our direction. August 1, 1990 was our target date, and we went about notifying employees and customers about our plan. I had taken an attitude of success in my life, and this was the first failure that I took so personally. There was within me a pity party of "Why me?" I was looking for someone or something to blame.

Question: Who turned on the light?

Answer:

Broke and broken on that morning of August 1, 1990, I left my home at dawn to take care of closing the doors of the restaurant. I remember feeling so alone and defeated, like every good thing to that point in my life was insignificant. I realized that a lot of what I was feeling was flesh, like what will people think? Where am I going to go? In fact a lot of stuff like that.

In route to the restaurant I approached a red light at an intersection. As I sat waiting for the green light, I noticed that someone had run down a phone booth with their vehicle, and the debris was scattered all over the street in front of me. I thought what a responsible person would do was to take a little time and clear the garbage from the road. Not really relishing getting started on the day's task of closing the restaurant, I chose to be responsible and clear the road. The phone booth had sat on the corner by a convenience store, so I gathered the remnants and placed them on the ground at that location. I turned to get in my car and heard a whisper from God in my head that said, "Go home, get your wife's camera and come back and take pictures of the phone booth." Knowing it was the Lords voice, I drove home, got the camera, returned, took the pictures, and dropped the film and the 24-hour Pay N Save film center and continued on to face the issues of the day. A few days later, I received a phone call from my wife asking why in the world I would take pictures of a broken down phone booth. I answered with the only explanation I had, which was, "The Lord told me to." She laughed and said the pictures will be on the kitchen counter when I got home. Later, I viewed the pictures and was surprised at what I saw. It appeared that the light was on in the booth, which seemed impossible because it was torn from its base, and all the wires were ripped out. As I tried to come up with an explanation, that same voice that told me to take the pictures spoke once more and said, "This imagery is to remind you that I am the light of your life, and as long as you concentrate on me (the light), darkness will flee." The immediate understanding I received was that everyone has broken dreams, disappointment, betrayal, and carnage around them that's wooing them away from the light (Jesus). He assured me that if I would concentrate on those things that keep my eyes and mind on Him, that carnage would pass, and victory would come. This was a simple directive by a God who is much bigger than my difficulties.

Jesus is the light, in Him there is no darkness.

(John 8:12)

Question: Who said, Get Down?

Answer:

In 1966 in Vietnam I was serving as a corporal in a sixteen-man squad. We had been whittled down to seven guys. We had a captain who had an idea of how to run our patrols and had decided that we would run our patrols once in the morning, one way, and once in the early evening the other way. It was about the second week of this patrolling method, and Charlie, the enemy, caught right on. So the first patrol went, came back, and saw nothing. I put the second patrol together, and we left and shortly walked right into an ambush, I mean they had as. Just before the shells went off I heard someone say, "Get down" in an audible voice. We hit the dirt and after a firefight fought our way out. When we returned I began the debriefing of my guys. De-briefing them is like an investigation of what each individual had experienced. I asked the first guy, "Did you holler, get down?" He said he did not, but that he heard me holler, "Get down." I went to the next guy, asked the same question and got the same answer. Ultimately, I found that all seven men reported the same thing, independent of each other. They did not hear any other voice but what they thought was my voice telling them, "Get down!" I was not saved at the time and the reality of that voice freaked me out. Little did I know how much God loved me and wanted me to know and love Him. He was there even before I knew Him.

Question: Is part of serving God taking chances on appearing weird or different?

Answer:

I was in the spaghetti factory having dinner, and I saw woman with who looked like her daughter eating in another area. I was just eaten by myself and God spoke to me and said, "Go to this woman and tell her that her thirty-one-year-old son, who is backslidden, will be back home within a month. She is not to stop praying, I hear her prayers. He will be back within thirty days." I was arguing with God and said that the word "backslidden" is such a Christian word, and if she's not a Christian it might not make sense to her. A son aged thirty-one? I'm thinking that's just too specific. What if she's not a Christian? I'm just concerned this lady might think I'm weird. So I'm playing these games with God, and then I say, "Okay God, she's really stoic so if you want me to do this please within the next thirty seconds have her break out in hysterical laughter just so I know it's you." Thirty seconds goes by; she doesn't laugh. I say, "Okay Lord, have her reach over and take a drink from her daughter's water cup." The Lord said, "Just trust me. You wanted me to use you, trust Me." So I walked over to her and I said, "This might sound really weird ma'am but I was praying and the Lord said that you have a son thirty-one years old who has backslidden, that he knew the Lord in earlier years, but he has chosen a different lifestyle. He also said that he has heard your prayers and your son will be back within thirty days and will rededicate his life to the Lord." She looked at me with tears in her eyes and said, "I have a thirty-one-year-old son. He was in the ministry and fell away. He's been away for seven years. He's an alcoholic, he lost his family, he lost his life, and my older son who is a believer and I have been praying ever since." She said, "Thank you. That word feels so right on, because everything feels so hopeless now." I don't know what happened because I never followed up with her but it was proof that God spoke to me.

Question: Should I step through that door?

Answer:

I was in junior high, twelve or thirteen years old and at a youth conference. I'd grown up in the church and went to a Christian school I had a lot of Bible knowledge but not a lot of spiritual fruit. I hadn't crossed the line and begun using all that I had learned in God's word. So I went to this youth conference; my sister was going to it so I decided I would go as well. The first day during one of the final worship times of the day, I was sitting with my eyes closed, and in my mind's eye I saw a door; it was just cracked open ever so slightly. God impressed on my heart saying, "Nick you've been on this side of the door for long enough. I've called you to use your background in church and your education in the Christian school. I want you to start using it and experiencing the full life I have for you." I was just amazed and just sat there pondering that call He had given me, and I said, "Okay God." And then I stepped through the door. I understood that I had the childhood and upbringing for purpose and that He wanted me to use it some way. So in my mind I saw myself walking through the door, and I realized there was a second door. I got through that door; there was another door and after that another. For as far as I could see there were doors. And God continued and said, "I'm always going to have your steps laid out for you and provide opportunity for you to use your life ahead of you for the Kingdom." I was filled with prompting to keep walking through the doors and amazed by the moment. It was vivid and real, and I can still remember it today as it was that first day.

Question: Can life change from destruction to construction?

Answer:

I'm Arnie, and I'm sixty-two years old. I had an extremely rough year in regard to my health. One Sunday in February 2009, in reaction to the health problems of which I had no apparent control, I determined to take my own life. As weird as it sounds I also felt I needed to go to church because it was communion. I went to the evening service knowing this was going to be my last communion. During that service there was a song a female vocalist was singing that began to speak to me in a way that never before happened. It was though she was singing directly to me and for me. It seemed we were the only two people in the room and that she was staring at me. The song was, "I Worship You Almighty God". I was not certain of what to expect; in fact, I really had no expectation. As I looked at her she changed into a radiant angel. Her change before my eyes gave me a moment of unidentifiable fear. Something was changing. However, I was still determined to complete my plan. I got up and ran to my car, drove to the bridge, which was to be my instrument of death. I had planned to jump from the bridge, but I was not emotional or fearful because the thought of death didn't scare me. As I approached the bridge a very clear voice spoke, the voice of God, said to me, "Fear not, I am here". With that every single thing that I was holding onto was lifted. I didn't think about death. I didn't think about jumping. My eyes were full of tears, and I was so appreciative that God grabbed a hold of my life through a song and his voice. I went home sobbing but totally understood that what I intended to do was not my call, that God was in control. I was not the control person I thought I needed to be. Since that day I have been thankful for each day He gives me and although not perfect, I spend time in the Word and prayer so that I might be used of Him.

SECTION FIVE:
THE BIBLE STANDS ALONE

Question: Is miracle healing for today?

Answer:

Somewhere in my mid-thirties, I got real serious about asking God this question. I had been receiving conflicting teachings on the subject. Some said, healing is for today, while others said it is not. I knew both groups were made up of sincere, loving believers. But I could not get away from the thought that if we are to pray and we are to lay hands on people for healing, and the Bible tells us to do that, then why would God have us do something or practice something that had no result? For that matter, why would we pray about anything if we did not believe that we had a God that would answer today? The bottom line for me was if miracle healing was for today, why would I not want to be part of that?

God had an answer.

One Friday night after a couple of hours sleep, I awoke and realized that I was praying in the Spirit, which was definitely unusual at that point of my spiritual journey. I only was awake for a few moments, but I experienced the same waking and praying on two more occasions. On the third occasion, about 3:00 a.m., I heard a gentle voice that I recognized inside me. This inner voice said, "Your wife has lung cancer. If you will lay hands on her and pray for healing in my name, she will be healed." Immediately I was confronted with doubts, because I had no knowledge of her disease and even though the voice was familiar, I had doubts in myself. After contemplating, it was my conclusion that I would respond to Jesus' leading, because after all it was what I had been seeking Him about recently. Laying my hands softly on my wife, I asked that Jesus would heal her from cancer and claimed it in His name. Strangely I didn't stay awake and think a lot about it because it seemed I was extremely tired. About 7:00 a.m. I awoke and found again as I did before that I was praying in the Spirit. I got up, washed my face, brushed my teeth, and went to the kitchen to begin my day. As I was deciding what to eat, that voice within me spoke again and said, "I want you to go to this location; there you will find an old man sitting on the curb. He will be stressed about a physical ailment, and if you will lay hands on him and pray for him in my name, he will be healed." I don't know about you, but I was not familiar with this kind of message from the Lord, direct and unobstructed. I thought perhaps I'd totally flipped and had real doubts about the authenticity of the voice, yet I knew the voice. I gave it some thought and logic told me, if it's God's voice then there will be an old man sitting on the curb. If it's not God's voice, he won't be there, and I will have to pray for healing and greater discernment. I jumped in my truck and drove to the area given to me by the voice. To my amazement, there was an old man sitting on the curb. After several attempts of trying to write this off as a coincidence, I decided there would be no harm in approaching this man to see if I could help. I approached him and asked if there was anything I could do. He began weeping and told me about some undiagnosed serious bleeding; he was sure he was dying, and he did not understand this because he had not completed the tasks God had given him and knew he was supposed to complete them. I told him I was not there by accident, that the Lord sent me, and further that if he would allow me to lay hands on him and pray for him that Jesus would heal him. He immediately said, "Oh yes!" I laid hands on him and prayed for him, and when I was finished I was led by the Spirit to explain that he was simply to go the doctor. The doctor would tell him he needed a minor procedure, and his problem would be gone. He accepted my prayers and instruction with thankfulness. I got into my truck and drove away. An awareness of fatigue came upon me. Immediately I began to pray in the Spirit and seek a greater understanding of what I had just experienced. On my way home, once again that inner voice said, "Before going home, I want you to go to this house, knock on the door, and inside there will be a man. If you lay hands on him and pray for him in my name, I will heal him." From the human side, knocking on a stranger's door at 8:00 on a Saturday morning was at the very least adventuresome. I drove to the house indicated and had decided on the way there that the worst that could happen was to have the door slammed in my face. To my surprise, a young pastor's wife, whom I've known for years, answered the door. "Ralph!" she said, and then asked, "How did you know we were back in town?" I said, I didn't know, and with really no other explanation asked if her husband Steve was home. She replied he was lying on the couch because he hasn't been feeling well, and would I like to see him? I said yes, and she led me to the living room where Steve was lying on the couch. Seeing me, he sat up, and I walked over and sat next to him. I was told in that gentle voice inside me, that Steve was not actually physically sick, but was suffering from a deep depression, and if I would lay hands on him and pray in Jesus name that this would be removed, and he would be healed. I explained to Steve why I was there and that I did not know who lived in this home when I knocked on the door. In fact, I had no idea that he had moved back from California. I said what I did know was that God had assured me that if I would lay hands on him he would be healed. He accepted both my explanation and my prayer. After some small talk I went away, again aware that I felt physically drained and somewhat mentally drained. It began to dawn on me that a loving Lord and Savior had answered my prayers about miracle healing for today in a miraculous way that I could not deny.

As I drove home, a strange exhaustion that was hitting me was explained to me by the Holy Spirit. He told me to recall what happened to Jesus in Mark 5:21–43.

The following bone is one of the first I collected. I was introduced to pastor Jason Hubbard by my daughter, Monique, who told me he had an amazing testimony. As a result of that encounter Jason has become a close and trusted friend and mentor who loves, seeks and serves our Lord.

Question: How can God reveal himself?

Answer:

The first time I heard God's audible voice I was thirty years old. This was in the spring of 2003. About 9:30 p.m., just before I was falling asleep, the presence of God began to fill up our bedroom. Then I heard God begin to speak in an audible voice for my first and only time. It sounded like thunder at first, and when the thunder came, it shook our bedroom so much that my wife came running in and thought it was an earthquake. Then He began to sound like rushing water, and then He spoke and said, "I want you to build a house of prayer for all nations, but first for the first nations." Obviously, I was trembling under the fear of God and didn't sleep much that night. The following morning I went to my church where we were in the middle of a five-day 24/7 prayer vigil for the dedication of our building to the Lord. Tim, Ken, and I were praying together at our appointed time of 4:30 a.m. Tim is one of the intercessors at the International House of Prayer (IHOP). That same night that God spoke to me an angel came and visited Tim in his bedroom. The angel handed him a scroll and said, "Tell Jason to name it, Light of the World Prayer Center," and then the angel left. The next morning when Tim and I met for prayer, I told him he would not believe what had happened to me in the night. I told him, and he filled me in with what had occurred with him. I started seeing lighthouses in vision form. I don't often see revelatory things like that, so this was a new thing for me. Each time I went to prayer I kept seeing lighthouses with the number 555 across the middle. I asked the Lord for a year—what 555 was. He never told me. Then on St. Patrick's day, Karen, who happened to be the group praying that day, called me up and said, "Jason I got this CD that you've got to listen to. Wes and Stacey Campbell were doing a worship conference over in Ireland at a place called Bangor Bay. They were asking God to restore a worship movement that had happened back in the sixth century, initially by St. Patrick then it continued to his descendants, St. Carabonis and St. Combo." She read me this information off the back of the CD cover. She said, "Jason this thing went on for 250 years, and scholars say it was one of the beginnings of the Irish European civilization. The arts, philosophy, everything was launched from this house of worship in the spirit of the tabernacle of David. So, they took the Psalms and prayed and sang those night and day for the 250 years." So she asked, "Jason guess when this movement started? It was 555 AD." I told her she had to be kidding. Then she said, "Guess what they called it? They called it The Light of the World Prayer Center." I thought to myself, that's amazing! I determined to learn more about this story. I had studied scriptural renewal movements at Regent College Seminary, and I hadn't heard of this Irish movement. I knew about Saint Patrick and the valley of the angels but never heard about this particular one before. I talked to someone and ended up getting the e-mail address of Matt Rightman, a worship leader over in England. Matt said, "Yeah, I wrote a song on this story." I also found out a guy named Ian Adamson, a scholar at Edinburgh (Scotland), who wrote a book on the story called *Light of the World*. I found the book, bought it, and had it sent to me from England. I opened it up to the first page, and the picture of the prayer and worship center looked just like the lighthouses I'd seen in my visions. I knew this was from the Lord. I found out a few years later from another one of our intercessory prayer people that, remember the Lord said house of prayer for all nations but first for the first Nations. It so happened that in1890 the U.S. government assigned numbers to all the tribal lands across the nation. The number that was assigned to the Nooksack Indian tribe, in our own backyard, was 555. I thought that was just unbelievable. Because of that, there is a primary mandate to build house of prayer centers to pray for all nations but first for the first Nations, the Native American nations. We continue to pray for the salvation of Israel and for revival to break out on tribal lands.

These tasks that were given to Jason wouldn't be possible without Jesus. They are happening because Jason is yielded to the leading of the Holy Spirit and keeps godly wise council around him at all times. He is a man of the Word and consumes it daily. In the past three years the Light of The World Prayer Center has been birthed, 24/7 prayer is happening and healing goes on. For information, go to www.lopc.org.

In the process of finishing this work, God reminded me of the greatest source of bones available to all, and instructed me as to how I was to deliver a few of those bones to you. With humble obedience and great joy I do as instructed. May they grow your faith as they have mine—may your light shine so that others might see your good works and glorify your Father who is in heaven.

Question: Will God do the impossible to get your attention?

Answer:

While walking on the beach the other day, I had the most unusual experience. I observed this very large fish—perhaps a whale beached itself—and vomited a man onto the sand. The man looked bleached and kept saying something like, this time I will do it your way Lord. This man's name was Jonah and a more complete account is recorded in the book of Jonah—chapters 1 –4.

Question: Why would a man build a boat on dry land?

Answer:

My father Shem tells of his father Noah, a just and godly man, whom God spoke to before the great flood. God stated that mankind was totally evil and that he was going to rid the earth of all men except Noah and his sons and their wives and children. He told him to build a great ark. The complete story is recorded in scripture. The book of Genesis chapters 6–9.

Question: What child was born to Mary in Bethleham?

Answer:

I ran into a highly educated man whose profession was astrology. One might refer to him as a wise king. He reported that he had followed a God star from afar to Bethlehem, he said there were other wisemen who had done the same. He went on and reported that sheppards had left their flocks because angels had visited them and told them of the birth of this holy child. All who came had an encounter with a God-child born of a woman named Mary. He said this Mary reported that she had not been with a man. Her husband-to-be Joseph confirmed this report and further testified that an angel had visited him and given instruction. It is my belief that this is all true. There is a written record of this entire occurrence in the scripture. It starts in Matthew 1:18 and goes on from there.

Question: Could this worker of miracles be Messiah?

Answer:

I am a servant who served at a wedding in Cana, and I must tell you of the most amazing thing I witnessed. Our master had not provided sufficient wine for the wedding so this man, Jesus of Nazareth, had us fill six eighteen to twenty-seven gallon jugs with water. Then after just moments He told us to ladle out some of the liquid and serve it to the ruler of the feast. The ruler tasted the water ,and it had been changed into fine wine. Since that time I have been following this Jesus and he has done many miracles. I do believe He is a great teacher sent by God or perhaps even the Messiah. This miracle and many more are recorded in the book of John chapter 2.

Question: Who wouldn't want this man to give a blessing on your meal?

Answer:

I was visiting my uncle the other day, and we attended a large gathering on the mountain side where a carpenter's son, Jesus the Nazarene, talked about the power and love of God. He spoke with great wisdom and authority only that which God can anoint. It was all quite an amazing experience. I was witness to a great miracle. His apostles, the twelve that have followed him, apparently fearing that the 5,000 people at the gathering might be getting hungry, asked Him if they should disperse the crowd so that they could find food. Instead, Jesus asked the apostles to bring to Him what food they could find, and they brought five loaves of bread and two fish. He blessed that meager amount of food and told them to distribute it to the crowd. After all those assembled had eaten and were full, Jesus had his apostles gather whatever food was leftover. The amount they picked up filled seven baskets. I was astonished! I would have found it hard to believe had I not witnessed it myself. The apostles reported that they also were amazed by this Jesus and that many believed, along with themselves, that He was Messiah. (For a more complete story of this incident, read Mark chapter six.)

Question: I believe this is the Christ; how about you?

Answer:

I have heard talk that Jesus, the man that was crucified instead of Barabbas, was totally innocent of all charges and could in fact be the Christ. You see I was a beggar, crippled from birth and could not stand or walk. Members of my family and friends would carry me each morning to the gate of the temple, the one called "beautiful," and I would beg for gifts of money and food. One afternoon as I was begging, two apostles of this man Jesus, Peter and John, came by and I asked them for alms. Peter said they had no money, but declared in the name of Jesus that I be healed and stand up and walk. With Peter's assistance, I arose and have been walking and leaping and praising God ever since. A complete record of my miracle and an even greater one for you is contained in chapter three of the book of the Acts of the Apostles. It will tell you the truth about this Nazarene.

CPSIA information can be obtained
at www.ICGtesting.com
Printed in the USA
FFOW03n0605050218
44896299-45106FF